Jamie Stilson is a Vineyard pastor wl
satisfaction when he is touching the lives of the disempowered,
the broken, the hurting. In *The Power of the Ugly*, Jamie speaks
their language while delivering a vital truth often missed in the
church: the *modus operandi* of God is most often to work through
weakness. The book combines a humor that will have you rolling
on the floor and a theology that is serious and engaging. I highly
recommend it, but only for the non-religious.

Bert Waggoner

National Director

Association of Vineyard Churches USA

* * *

Jamie Stilson is an ugly man. And I mean that in the nicest
way possible. To understand what I mean, you need to read his
revolutionary and well-written piece. In France they erect placards
and advertisements on bus shelters every Easter-time that say
'The Grace of God is Folly' (obviously, in French!). That slogan
captures something very New Testament, very Gospel, very Jesus.
And in his book *The Power of Ugly* Jamie Stilson expounds on that
Folly, that Grace, and our utter and eternal dependence on it, and
makes it all memorable with his hilarious stories (when I think of
him in future, I will always be assailed with a mental image of him
in his tighty-whities — ugly!)

This book has the potential to become a new classic on the
subject of Grace. Grace for life; Grace for relationships; Grace for
ministry; Grace for adversity and persecution; Grace to counteract
the pressure of a consumerist approach to church and the Christian
life. Using Biblical story and text with the honesty I have always

known him for, Jamie shows us how the real folly is to subscribe to standards of 'pretty' and polished, how pastors are dying on their feet because of the imposition on them of a yoke that Jesus did not design, and how discovering fresh freedom from the inside out is an urgent pursuit if we are going to survive for the long haul and stay sane.

The Power of Ugly cuts close to the bone. It explores religious paradigms and pokes fun at Christian mythology in words without religious frills. Jamie expresses himself in words that might offend some, but the offence is essential if we are to get the message. The strength and passion of his message is a sledge-hammer that breaks through a musty, stifling cellar of lies we've all believed, and lets in God's fresh air. Every prospective pastor should read it; every jaded, burned-out pastor should read it; everyone exhausted by the legalisms of the church should make it their new devotional read for the year; everyone who wants a sound reason to break away from the plastic, image-conscious, performance-driven picture of ministry should read it. Read it and laugh at yourself in Jamie. Read it and weep. Read it and let yourself off the hook. Just read it!"

Costa Mitchell
National Director
Association of Vineyard Churches
South Africa

* * *

Jamie Stilson pulls back the veil on the ugliness of our lives and powerfully reminds us of the love of a beautiful God ... even in our ugliness. Jamie never takes him self or life too seriously, but he is very serious about hurting people. Jamie reminds us of God's tender heart for hurting people. *The Power of Ugly* will stir your heart as it shakes you out of the paradigm you are living in to see God, people and the church in an "ugly" new way. Prepare to let God change you as Jaime opens the world of ugly.

Jeff Swearingen
Founding Pastor
Crosspoint Christian Church
Cape Coral Florida

*   *   *

I once read this, "Friendship is like a prism through which the many variations of beauty are revealed in our lives." Jamie Stilson has been one of those great friends ever since I first met him nearly twenty-five years ago. But in this case, he has been the kind of friend that has helped reveal the "ugly" in my own life. Whether traveling to Africa together or just doing lunch together every Monday for the last fourteen years, Jamie has shown me how to take God seriously without taking myself too seriously. Jamie has helped me to see my own ugliness and my need of God's humbling grace. I absolutely loved reading his book, *The Power of Ugly*, because it so represents who he is-authentic, earthy, funny, insightful and in love with Jesus. This is a must read. You will laugh and you will cry. You will be challenged and you will be blessed. For sure, you will get a fresh new view of your ugly self and of God's beautiful grace.

Dennis Gingerich
Founding Pastor
Cape Christian Fellowship
Cape Coral, Florida

*   *   *

For more than fourteen years, it has been my delight and joy to do life richly and deeply with Pastor Jamie Stilson and the Vineyard Community Church of Cape Coral. In that time, both pastor and people have championed a community of ugly grace. They have modeled the kingdom reality that the local church is not a gathering of the already convinced, but a lighthouse for the broken and marginalized. This book will give you a flavor of The Power of Ugly they embody!"

Jorge Acevedo
Lead Pastor
Grace United Methodist Church
Cape Coral, Florida

* * *

The Power of ugly:

a celebration of earthy spirituality

Jamie J. stilson

HARMON
PRESS

The Power of Ugly: A Celebration of Earthy Spirituality
by Jamie J. Stilson

HARMON
PRESS

Published by:
Harmon Press
Woodinville, WA 98077
http://www.harmonpress.com

ISBN: 978-1-935959-02-1

Library of Congress Control Number: 2010938630

Cover Photo by Kim Stilson
Cover Design by Jasen Williams

To Kim,
my bride and my best friend,

To Kelly, Kristy, and Kasey,
three daughters who have taught me to have the Father's heart.

To John Wimber,
you modeled the Power of Ugly to me.

Contents

Prologue. Ugly Birth

Scat Happens

After another tough Sunday at church, I reluctantly answered the ringing phone, praying that it was not another person bent on draining the last dregs of my energy. All I wanted to do at that moment was to kick back on the couch and watch some trashy violent movie. The caller announced himself as Bert Waggoner, the national director of the Vineyard churches. I have been part of the Vineyard since its early days, and no national leader had ever called me before — so I was nervous to say the least. I had seen Bert two days earlier and had sheepishly given him a rough manuscript of this book and asked him to read it if he had time.

Now Bert was speaking on the other end of the phone, "Jamie, I am going to have to kick you out of the Vineyard."

My heart sank, and before I could ask why, he went on to tell me that he'd read my manuscript on the plane ride back to Houston, and that it had caused him to "laugh so hard that I hurt body parts!"

Bert encouraged and affirmed me in my new venture in writing. The thought that the Lord had used the book to minister to a national leader who had faithfully weathered many storms at the helm of our denomination was comforting. He told me he had read it while traveling to deal with a mess involving a fallen church leader, and the idea that this book ministered to him fulfilled my prayers for it.

My heart's desire is to encourage and refresh those who faithfully serve the Lord, as well as to plant seeds of hope in those who are still uncertain about Jesus. There's truth to the cliché that laughter is medicine — it opens people to God's truth. Just as the great theologian, Mary Poppins, taught us, "A spoonful of sugar helps the medicine go down." Life is so hard and filled with so much pain — especially for those called to walk with people as a shepherd through their dark valleys, while struggling through their own gloomy nights. I offer this book to you as a cup of cold water in the name of the Lord (Mark 9:41). I pray that *The Power of Ugly* will cause you to lighten up, to laugh, and to learn something.

This book is my Isaac — the Birth of Laughter. Isaac was born to Abraham and Sarah during their old age.[1] God had promised them a child, and after years of barrenness, they felt that God needed their help, so they devised a plan to conceive a child through one of their servant girls. Their plan succeeded, and they had a son named Ishmael. The only problem was that God did not approve of this, and he told them that their child would come directly from both of them. They laughed at the thought of two elderly people conceiving. God told them that because they laughed, their son would be named Isaac, which means *he laughs*. Every time they called their son's name, "Isaac," they would laugh and be reminded that nothing is impossible with God. Ishmael had been the fruit of their self-effort — the achievement of human strength and the power of beauty. Isaac was a grace baby — conceived by the will of God in spite of mortal limitations and weaknesses. These limitations and weaknesses are what I mean when I talk about The Power of Ugly.

I discovered The Power of Ugly after many failed attempts at

---

1. An old man once described his intimacy with his wife to me by comparing it to "shooting pool with a rope." See Genesis 12-21 for the full story of God's promise to Abraham and Sarah.

helping God produce his promises for my life and ministry by using The Power of Jamie. I have birthed so many Ishmaels. Now that the Father has given me my Isaac, I join with Sarah in saying, "... God has brought me laughter, and everyone who hears about this will laugh with me" (Gen 21:6). Who would have thought that God could use a flawed man like me to demonstrate the power of his grace? This book is a celebration of that grace revealed through my ugliness. My only boast in this book is in my weaknesses, providing plenty of holes for the power of the grace of God to shine through on every page.

The Power of Ugly in many ways fulfills the same mission of a forgotten Jesuit Priest whose ministry ended in complete failure. Benedetto de Goes was sent on a mission in 1602 with two goals: the first was to discover the lost empire of Cathay that had supposedly been discovered centuries earlier by Marco Polo; the second was to find an overland link between India and China so the gospel could be spread. After three years and three thousand miles, Goes sent back his only report in a very understated and stoic assessment, "The journey is very long, full of difficulties and dangers. No one from the Society [of Jesus] should attempt to repeat it."[2] His body was never found, and he failed to discover a new empire confirming that China and Cathay were the same. He did not have a glorious discovery like that of Columbus — discovering a new world and putting the Americas on the map. In fact, Goes actually removed a place from the map — Cathay. He discovered what was not there and proclaimed *do not take this path*! That is one ugly mission.

This is what I am doing in Ugly. I am removing false ideas of what it means to be spiritual from the religious map. I am crying out "do not take this path" based on my own failures. The failed mission of Benedetto de Goes resulted in saving many lives of his

---

2. Chris Lowney, *Heroic Leadership* (Chicago, IL: Loyola Press, 2003), 71.

fellow priests; and in this way, his mission was a great success. That is The Power of Ugly: God taking our weakness and failures and birthing something beautiful from them.

There are many people that have helped Ugly be birthed. The first is my wife, Kim, who has served beside me for thirty-three years. My daughters, who have shared the whole Ugly journey with dad. Katie for deciphering my unknown tongues as I hand wrote the first draft. Jasen and Caleb for your tireless hours and piles of pork eaten at Rib City as you helped Ugly become what it is, you young guys make me have to get up earlier just to keep up. All of my staff: Naomi, Charles, David, Jasen, Caleb; and the church counsel: Mark, Troy, Chuck, and Katie. My editor Alice Peck who took a risk on a rookie. My family at the Cape Coral Vineyard Community Church, which has been the soil that the principles in Ugly have grown out of, you are a beautiful group of people who are making a difference in this world.

I want to say a special thanks to Bubba the Black Bear for providing the scat in the backyard of our cabin. The flower is God's miracle of regeneration, which serves as a fresh reminder of The Power of Ugly: that grace grows best in the messy places of our lives. Kim took the photograph, which we like to call "scat happens," and so does grace.

I hope you will laugh with me as I take you on a journey into the mess, the scat of my life. You will witness the flower of his grace growing out of the fertile soil of my weaknesses. I pray that as you read this ugly book you will experience the "Birth of Laughter," so that I can avoid the consequences that a wise person[3] warned about, "If you are going to tell people the truth, you'd better make them laugh, otherwise, they'll kill you."

---

3. This quote is disputed. It may be from W. C. Fields, George Bernard Shaw, or Charlie Chaplin.

We live in a world full of people struggling to be, or at least to appear, strong, in order not to be weak; and we follow a gospel which says that when I am weak, then I am strong. And this gospel is the only thing that brings true healing.
— N. T. Wright

Chapter 1. Ugly Beauty

Like a Gold Ring in a Pig's Nose

I can still hear the words of Hank Williams Jr. ringing in my ears, as he shouted out, "Are you ready for some football? A Monday night party!" followed by the voice of the announcer declaring, "This is Monday Night Football, with Howard Cosell, Frank Gifford and Dandy Don Meredith."

It was sometime in the '80s, and I had settled into my lazy boy for an evening of armchair quarterbacking. I don't remember who was playing that night, but I will never forget the beautiful woman in the stands. It seems that producers don't think men can stay interested in a football game without constantly panning the crowd for hot babes; and this night the camera landed on a real beauty queen. She must have spent hours at the salon, hoping to be noticed on national TV, and tonight was her lucky night!

As the camera zoomed in on her, Dandy Don, who was known to be quite the ladies man, could not help from breathing heavy.[1] As Dandy Don took the opportunity to fire off some suggestive comments, the pretty girl ever so gracefully raised her hand, in a very ladylike manner, to scratch her upper lip. Then, without

---

1. This was before video screens were installed in football stadiums. She had no idea she was on TV screens across America, in front of millions of people. (On this night, the nation got a glimpse of this beauty queen without her awareness.)

warning (once she discerned the coast was clear), she inserted her perfectly manicured bright red fingernail deep into her nose. She was not scratching, she was digging — deeper and deeper — on the hunt for a big, juicy booger lodged somewhere in the recesses of her nostril! The camera couldn't pull away quickly enough, trying to save her from national exposure and embarrassment. Never at a loss for words, Dandy Don, keeping with football imagery, inquired, "I wonder if she scored?"[2]

I laughed so hard I fell out of my chair! Monday Night Football had just given America an incredible gift. It was unedited, unpolished, and certainly not airbrushed. It was just raw, Ugly Beauty. Not evil, bad, or wrong — only nasty reality. This woman went from alluring to ugly in the time it took to pick her nose. The world wants to sell us on a beauty that is artificial — with no flaws, blemishes, or ugliness; no wrinkles, warts, dimples, smells, hang ups, or weaknesses — fake beauty. This story makes me think of the wisdom of a man who "knew" more women than Hugh Hefner:

"Like a gold ring in a pig's snout is a beautiful woman who shows no discretion."[3]

This is the context I want to give the word *ugly* in this book. Not as it is often used — to speak of acts that are morally repugnant, violent, or evil. I want to talk about ugly meaning raw, real, broken, flawed, weak, smelly, and yes, sticky. Not pretty. Ugly is a description of real, honest humans. A pig is ugly (but they

---

2. The camera managed to pull away before we discovered if she had accomplished her mission. Or did she have to sing, along with Bono, "I still haven't found what I'm looking for"?

3. These are the words of King Solomon in Proverbs 11:22. According to 1 Kings 11, Solomon had over 700 wives and 300 concubines — you could say he knew women. The woman he describes in this proverb is shallow, empty-headed, and has no character.

sure make great ribs!) and putting a beautiful ring in its snout does not change what it is; it's a vain attempt to disguise the truth of ugliness. Conversely, a beautifully manicured fingernail with a nasty booger on it does not destroy real beauty — it just keeps it real.

Our society worships people that are beautiful but often artificial. They nip and tuck, Botox and barf, ingest and implant whatever it takes to be strong, skinny, and sexy. And yet we scrutinize their lives with a magnifying glass, seeking any signs of weakness or imperfection that we can expose.

A few days ago I was standing in the checkout line at the grocery store and one of those "intellectually stimulating" magazines caught my eye. On the cover was a blown-up picture of some movie star's butt hanging out of her bathing suit. Some fatty dimples on her thighs were circled and a line pointed to the question "Whose fat butt is this?" It could have been mine! How sad, how shallow, how vain — no wonder our culture creates people with eating disorders.

There are exceptions, but they are rare. As I write this book, Susan Boyle is the phenomenon *du jour*. If you are unaware, she was a contestant on the British version of *American Idol*. Susan, according to one newspaper article, is an:

> ...unglamorous, unfashionable, and unknown [woman who] faced down a sneering British audience and panel of judges on *Britain's Got Talent,* including the ever-sneering Simon Cowell. Then, in an instant, she turned jeers to cheers with her rendition of one of the weepier numbers from Les Misérables. Almost as instantly, Boyle went viral: A clip on YouTube garnered millions of hits .... All of us reveled in the fact that even in our image-managed world, we could still have the tables turned on us."[4]

The article goes on to describe responses to Susan as,

---

4. Maria Puente, "Why Susan Boyle Inspires Us," *USA Today*, April 20 2009.

"vindication… surprise… [bringing] guilt … [and] shame. Boyle forced people to recognize how often they dismiss or ignore people because of their looks… 'Is Susan Boyle ugly? Or are we?' asked essayist Tanya Gold in Britain's *The Guardian*."[5]

Boyle was the youngest of nine children, is learning-disabled, was mocked as a girl, and had never been kissed. She is just a choir singer from Scotland; but she has something that the world can only scratch their heads and wonder about — true beauty! Hidden in that "ugly" package is the presence and true beauty of God.

Yes, every now and then God gives the world a glimpse of his wonder through a flawed human vessel. Yet most of the world misses it, thinking Susan Boyle is just a homely woman who sings well — but that could never touch hearts and produce such strong emotions. This is The Power of Ugly. It is God turning the tables on us. What we call beautiful is often called ugly by God, and what we call ugly, he often sees as beautiful.

Christians are not exempt from revering the wrong kind of beauty. We want pretty churches where everyone is full of love and kindness. We look for perfect pastors who are like Superman married to Mother Theresa with little angels for children. We expect perfect sermons that are not too long and that help us discover the secrets to a painless, problem-free, best life *now*.

These Christians worship a nice, safe, and pretty Jesus. There is no room for ugly, weak people who struggle, fail, sin, and pick their noses. Christian books and worship music are produced by spiritual superstars that are smart, successful, and magazine cover-ready. If they ever did have any sins and failures, they happened "years ago," and off camera. These superstars appear to be worthy enough to tell the rest of us ugly people how to get our lives together. They tell us how to be spiritual and successful, spiritual

---

5. Ibid.

and happy, spiritual and good-looking. They want to share their "secret" with us so that we can be thin and victorious like they are. The sad reality is that what they present as truths are often gold rings in the noses of people who remain ugly. If you scratch just a little deeper you will discover the real and nasty secret that all of these "Spiritual Giants" are flawed, struggling, sinful, weak, insecure, (normal) humans — just ugly people in need of God's grace.

Our attempts to make Christianity look appealing to a watching world have had the opposite effect. People can see through our vain attempts to hide our ugliness better than we can! This endeavor to glamorize our spirituality is a form of what one of my favorite authors, Eugene Peterson, calls "ecclesiastical pornography."[6] He wrote about how this type of spirituality flaunts the strength and beauty of people in a vain attempt to be relevant and attractive to the world. This promotion of Ugly Beauty — beauty that is shallow, fake, and full of gold rings — actually has the opposite effect, because it keeps Christians from reaching a hurting world with real truth. Broken people are not looking for pretty people to tell them how ugly they are or how they need to become pretty. They're looking to be accepted and loved unconditionally.

Many years ago, I went to a church service to see the World's Strongest Man. All those muscles and a Christian, too! We'd finally found someone we could brag about. He could bend nails with his teeth and lift a table with seven men on it. At the beginning of each service, the church had people share stories of how they found Jesus through watching the World's Strongest Man. Everyone was shocked when this young, handsome athlete shared that what brought him to Jesus was listening

---

6. Peterson, Eugene. *Under the Unpredictable Plant*. Grand Rapids: Eerdmans, 1992. 22.

to a young girl talk about how, as a paraplegic confined to a wheelchair, she would tell her friends about how Jesus made her strong and gave her joy. He did not need to be impressed by the message of the World's Strongest Man; he needed to see the beauty of ugliness — grace shining through the weakness of a young girl.

Only as we learn to celebrate the beauty of ugliness will the real beauty of God be visible to the world we are trying to reach. Our own beauty and strength will never save those who need Christ. You can keep wearing your gold rings, but we know a secret about you — you are ugly just like everybody else.

Our porno pictures of Christianity offer us false illusions. They are sad, shallow substitutes for the true beauty of the church, Jesus, and his grace. We will discover in this book that the strength of humanity, the beauty of humanity, and even the goodness of humanity will never reveal the Beauty of God, which can only be seen through Jesus working through our ugliness. The Apostle Paul said it this way:

> "... Therefore I will boast all the more gladly about my weaknesses, so that ... Christ's power may rest on me" (2 Cor 12:9, emphasis added).

He was determined to brag only about his struggles, weaknesses, and failures so that the beauty of God's grace could be revealed through his life. This is The Power of Ugly.

After all, if mere beauty, strength, or goodness could save people, why would Jesus have wasted his life dying on a bloody cross?

*　*　*

This book is like Gnosticism in reverse. Gnosticism was an early church heresy that, in various forms, is still with us today. The Gnostics believed the human body was evil and that you found salvation through a secret knowledge — called *gnosis* — which certain people had acquired through special revelations from spirit beings. The Gnostic saw all physical things as evil and taught that the only real beauty was spirit. They viewed the body as something that hindered the spirit and needed to be escaped from through either *gnosis* or the death of the body.

In *The Power of Ugly*, there is a hidden ugly secret knowledge that you might miss if you do not have the eyes to see it. Without a special revelation of ugliness, you might read this book as raw, crude, simple stories about some guy who screws up a lot, is often caught with his pants down (literally), and is unable to write without displaying symptoms of ADD. Here is a clue to help you discover the secret hidden in this book: it lays buried under a nasty pile of humanity — my ugliness.

It is my prayer that the simple, earthy stories recorded in this book will give hope to weak people. I pray that you can discover The Power of Ugly in your life. I hope the celebration of my ugliness will encourage you to not allow your ugliness stop you from getting in the game. So come jump in, and start singing, praying, laughing, and celebrating your ugly story.

You could say that this is my mission from God in this book: to lift up my voice — and, on occasion, pull down my pants — calling people to celebrate their ugliness. Being ugly is easy; just throw away your gold rings and celebrate being you.

* * *

Warning: Discovering The Power of Ugly will cost you your pride as you learn to take off your religious fig leaves and stand butt-naked[7] before God, being honest about your weaknesses and

---

7. Or as they say in South Africa, "Kaalgat."

confessing your sins. You'll have to stop hiding your scars and failures and start celebrating them! So burp, pass gas, and pick your nose. You are human, and yes, you are flawed, weak, and ugly, which is no surprise to God. Becoming a follower of Jesus does not remove all your ugliness. In fact, offering your ugliness to Jesus allows him to cover it with the beauty and power of his grace. So lighten up and learn to laugh at yourself. Nothing offends a prideful, religious mindset more than people who love to laugh, especially when they are laughing at themselves.

There can be no healing until one becomes aware of being sick. Jesus said it this way: "... It is not the healthy who need a doctor, but the sick" (Mark 2:17). So, Dr. Jesus came only to heal sick people; he has no cure to offer those who think that they are already whole.

We need to learn from the life of John the Baptist, who had the honor of introducing Jesus to the world as the "... Lamb of God, who takes away the sins of the world" (John 1:29)

John referred to himself simply as a "voice" (John 1:23), knowing that only Jesus is the Word of God. John's prayer and life passion — which needs to become ours — was "He must increase, but I must decrease" (John 3:30, KJV). The opposite of this is the false power of beauty: the more you increase in your own strength, beauty, and success; the more Jesus will shrink, until, before you know it, you think you are God.

God loves ugly. In fact, he only loves ugly. Jesus only died for ugly people. Amazing Grace only saves ugly people. There is no hope to offer you if you think you are near perfect and better than others, as you stand there with a beautiful gold ring hanging from your nose. The Bible warns us that, "... God opposes the proud but gives grace to the humble" (Jas 4:6) — the ugly.

We live in a world that celebrates superficial beauty and rejects ugly, yet God sees beauty in all of us despite our ugliness. Jesus loves us just the way we are. So if you feel your ugliness disqualifies you from making a difference in this world, then this book is for you. Come along with this ugly writer and laugh with me as we celebrate The Power of Ugly. You may discover that ugly is the new beautiful!

The Power of Ugly

Where there is laughter,
Jesus is always near.
Where there are tears,
He is quick to appear.

But where there is pride,
He is sure to hide.
Where this is pretending,
There will be no mending.

Where there is weakness,
His Grace is perfected.
And when he finds ugly,
His beauty is reflected.

....

I know of only two alternatives to hypocrisy:
perfection or honesty.
— Philip Yancey

Chapter 2. Ugly Jamie

Tighty-Whities

"Let's do it!" Off went the clothes and we were left with only the masks covering our faces. Like Indian warriors — without the buckskins — we headed off to battle. The enemy was gathered at a nearby house; a party we were not cool enough to get invited to. We crashed through the hedge into the backyard where fifty of our classmates were drinking and partying. We were greeted with screams and cheers as the shock and awe of seven butt-naked boys set in. What a rush it was to make such a shocking entrance; we felt so manly. It was such a thrill to be able to disrupt and mock those who ignorantly left us out.

We were on a mission from God — that is, until my bare foot struck a hidden sprinkler head. I went down like I had been shot! My first sensation was extreme pain, wondering if I had broken my toes. This was followed quickly by an overwhelming sense of embarrassment as I felt the peering eyes of the crowd gathered around this fallen warrior. I was quickly comforted by the thought that my fellow streakers, hidden safely behind their masks, would return to pick up their fallen comrade. They, however, turned out to be no Army Rangers; I was forsaken, alone, and naked on the ground in front of my classmates.

When you were a kid did you ever have those terrible nightmares where you found yourself in the classroom with only your underwear on? You didn't want to make a move, as you hoped no one would notice you were nearly naked. All you could do was try to figure out how you got in there with no one noticing you, so you could attempt to escape the same way. Those were deep fears!

Take that nightmare, remove the underwear, and add fifty of your peers. My only hope of anonymity was in the mask I was wearing. As I laid there with my toes throbbing, I comforted myself with the lie "at least no one will know it's me." That illusion was quickly shattered when someone shouted, "It's Jamie!" All I could do was lay there as they pointed, laughed, and hurled mocking comments assaulting my manhood.[1]

So what do you do when your mask has been removed and you have been humiliated before a merciless crowd? Do you cry for mercy, hoping some kind soul will give you their shirt? Do you just get up and tell them all to go f*** themselves? Or do you just limp away, still trying to act cool (covering your shame behind a mask)?

* * *

For reasons known only to God, he has chosen to make my life a parable of the beauty of ugliness. In fact, most of my staff at our church, and most of my close friends, have had the blessed experience of seeing Jamie in his tighty-whities.[2] I'll give you one example of these horrendous encounters.

---

1. This was the '70s, years before *Seinfeld*, so I could not even quote George who was similarly caught with his pants down in front of a young lady after he had taken a very cold swim. As she pointed and laughed, he screamed in defense of his manhood, "It's shrinkage!" With all the strength I could muster, I stood up, wishing I had a fig leaf like Adam's to hide my shame; while in reality, a four-leaf clover might have done the trick.

2. Many have seen more than that. Those that have only seen the pastor in his tighty-whities should feel lucky. Warning: you might also get initiated into this ugly club if you make it through this book.

My staff and some of my family had just wrapped up a week at a church conference, so we took some time off at a cabin in the Tennessee mountains. We arrived at this beautiful place with great expectations of rest and retreat. This was quickly interrupted when Kim, my wife, screamed, "It's a scorpion!" She had discovered a large, vicious looking creature in the kitchen. Shortly after, there was another scream, "There's another one in this bedroom!" We all went into battle mode, searching the entire house and putting these evil intruders to death. Wisdom at that point would have been to pack up and find a hotel, but I was too cheap and macho to let some little bugs drive me out. I assured Kim that we had destroyed them all and the cabin, according to my expert opinion, was now safe. As we struggled to get to sleep that first night, I remember my wife whispering fearfully in the dark to me, "I don't have a good feeling about this house." We tossed and turned all night, worrying about some vicious scorpion that might be climbing into bed with us.

In the middle of the night, right after we had finally settled into a sound slumber, Kim and I were startled awake by a violent crash. It had come from upstairs where the rest of our group was sleeping. Reacting without thinking, I jumped out of bed, and was pounding up the stairs when suddenly there was a second, louder crash. I was certain that it was either a bear that had smashed through the roof, or an intruder who was after my five-year-old granddaughter Kally (who Gramps calls his "Sweet Love"). I was ready to take on whatever was attacking my granddaughter, even if it was a giant scorpion — like something out of a Steven King novel. There was certainly no time to put on clothes, so I was headed to battle with only my tighty-whities on.[3]

---

3. I have never had a body you would want to put on a swimsuit calendar; and the older I get, the worse it looks. One time I was walking on a California

I threw the door to the upstairs room open and slammed on the light switch, ready to die fighting for my loved ones, only to discover that the first crash was actually "Sweet Love" falling out of bed onto the wood floor. The larger second crash was her mother, who, instinctually jumped out of bed to come to her daughter's aid and had, in the darkness of this strange environment, run straight into the wall. On the way down, she had also smashed her big toe on the bedpost and ripped off a toenail!

So there I stood in my tighty-whities, fists balled up, breathing heavy from adrenaline and the flight up the stairs, ready to do battle. Meanwhile, Caleb, our student pastor, lay as still as a corpse on the top bunk with the sheets pulled up to his nose.[4] Rylee, Caleb's future wife, was on another bunk staring at the mostly-naked guy that she calls her pastor.[5] My wife, who is never going to be a nurse, arrived on the scene moments later (after having wisely taken an extra moment to put on a nightgown). She began attempting to fix up our daughter's bleeding toe and went into the bathroom to get a wet towel. Suddenly, we heard a third crash, and from where I was standing I could only see my wife's legs sticking out from the bathroom into the hallway. Kim had passed out, overwhelmed by all the blood.

---

beach with some friends (we were fully clothed). A jogger — a man who had steroids written all over him — ran by in a Speedo. He had a much younger bikini babe at his side (and she was more implants than reality). In all of my out-of-shape ugliness I looked him straight in the eye and said, "you know, man, I will have a body like you at the resurrection!" He looked at me as though I had slapped him. He didn't know whether to stop and fight me, or to thank me for the complement; so they just continued on bouncing down the beach.

4. Caleb later reported that he was in great fear of me at that moment, knowing that I was there to hurt somebody. He hid safely under the covers, just thinking "This is going to be an ugly journey doing ministry with Jamie."

5. Rylee was probably in fear and just wondering, "Could my future husband turn into something like Ugly Jamie?"

"Sweet Love" was on the ground still crying from her fall. Her mom was crying over her big toe. Nurse Kim was peacefully passed out on the bathroom floor. The other two freaked-out staff members were staring at an ugly fat guy in his underwear looking to kill someone. This is how you get in the inner circle of leadership in our church.

*   *   *

There is a story in the eighth chapter of the Gospel of John about a woman caught in the act of adultery with a married man. And if that wasn't bad enough, the people who caught her were some of the religious leaders in her town. The man she was having sex with was probably another one of the religious leaders — who probably received a "free pass" from his friends — so they only brought the woman, still naked, and threw her at the feet of Jesus. These leaders didn't care much about the morality of the situation; they were trying to set a trap for Jesus. According to Old Testament law, a man and woman caught in adultery could be put to death (Lev 20:10), but Jesus had been going around preaching a message of love, grace, and forgiveness. If Jesus did not uphold the Law, he would not be acting justly; but if he agreed to stone her, he would not be acting lovingly. They had set the trap, but they were about to fall into it themselves.

Jesus bent over and began drawing in the sand. We don't know what he wrote; we only know the effect that it had on these men. They had rocks in their hands, prepared to stone the woman to death, but one by one (starting with oldest) they dropped their stones and began to walk away, being "... convicted by their own conscience" (John 8:9, KJV).

Whatever Jesus wrote in the sand had torn off their self-righteous religious masks. They had stumbled on a sprinkler and were lying as naked as the woman before Jesus. This would have opened the doors for the possibility of their own healing if they had taken the opportunity to come to the Light, but instead they chose to limp away, still hiding behind their masks. Jesus said, "... If any one of you is without sin, let him be the first to throw a stone at her" (John 8:7). Some translations have Jesus saying, "If any one of you is without *this* sin, let him be the first to throw a stone at her." Whether it is any sin, or this particular one, Jesus is giving permission to the perfect ones, the ones who aren't ugly, to become the judges, jury, and executioners.[6]

Some have suggested that Jesus was writing the Ten Commandments in the sand with the same finger that originally wrote them on the stones for Moses (Ex 32:16). Then, no one in the crowd could pass the test, which asked the question, "Who has not broken one of these?" That may be true, but there is another theory. I think that Jesus, who knows all men's hearts, wrote the names of the women that these self-righteous leaders had committed adultery with (some physically, others by fantasizing — both are guilty according to Matthew 5:28). Can you imagine the hush that came over this judgmental crowd as Jesus wrote in the dirt the name Bertha, pausing, because everyone knew that old Benjamin the Pharisee was sleeping with her. Benjamin had just hit a sprinkler and gone down hard in butt-naked shame — with his mask torn off.

You can hear the younger ones snickering, thinking they were safe behind their masks and religious fig leaves until ... Jesus wrote Wilma ... Connie ... Martha. One after another, they dropped their rocks and walked away, heads hanging in shame. Not one fell to his knees in honest humility to confess, "I am just as guilty as

---

6. This is why in our ugly church, we warn people that we "do not allow perfect people to attend." See Chapter 9.

this woman." Not one begged Jesus for mercy. They all continued believing the lie — that masking their sins was the cure — instead of coming to the Light to be healed and forgiven.

At the sound of each stone dropping, hope began to fill the heart of the guilty and shamed woman lying naked at the feet of God. After all of her accusers had dropped their condemning stones and left, only Jesus stood before her. As she looked up into the face of God, into his eyes of love, he asked her "Where are they? Has no one condemned you?" (John 8:10).[7] "No one has," she replied, with the implication: *Only you are left.* Only Jesus remained standing before her as Judge. Jesus — the only one who had passed the Big Ten Test. The only one who had never sinned. The only perfect one who could justly throw stones to kill her. What would he do?

The words Jesus spoke next are the heart of the gospel; they are the heart of God. "... Neither do I condemn you ... go now and leave your life of sin" (John 8:11). With these words I am convinced Jesus took off his coat and gave it to her, to cover the shame of her nakedness. God, in the Garden of Eden, did the same thing for Adam and Eve when he killed the first animal as a sacrifice to secure coats to cover over their shame and nakedness (Gen 3:21). This first death serves as an ugly, but beautiful, picture. Ugly because death is a violation, a bloody terror, a painful loss — it is unfair. Beautiful because it is filled with hope and promise, pointing to the ultimate sacrifice of God's "... one and only son, that whoever believes in him shall not perish but have eternal life" (John 3:16). This ugly/ beautiful sacrifice in the garden provided cover for the guilty, just as the sacrifice of Jesus would provide an eternal covering that removes all of our shame, guilt, fear, pain, and ugliness.

---

7. Condemned could also be translated "accused."

Jesus may have covered her with his coat, but soon he would be that perfect sacrifice that would cover her shame forever. As the old hymn "On Christ the Solid Rock," by Edward Mote reminds us:

> Dressed in His righteousness alone,
> faultless to stand before His throne.
> On Christ the solid rock I stand;
> all other ground is sinking sand,
> all other ground is sinking sand.

The words Jesus spoke to the woman brought new life to her and will do the same to all who give up on trying to hide from God — wearing masks to cover their own ugliness. Jesus did not love this woman because she was perfect, flawless, and beautiful. No, he loved her, and loves all of us, in spite of our ugliness. He covers us in the beauty of his grace. Out of love, he chose to provide an everlasting covering for all of our shame and ugliness. The price that he paid for this choice was suffering on the cross as he hung naked, mocked by the very people he had created.

We are always presented with a choice: remove our masks and expose all of our secrets and ugliness to come to the light for healing (John 3:18), or continue hiding from God behind our fig leaves and masks. How is that mask working for you?

* * *

From the beginning in the Garden of Eden, after what is called the fall of man in Genesis 3, humans have been trying to hide the shame they feel because of their sin. Adam and Eve disobeyed God and their eyes were "opened" (Gen 3:7). They then saw each other for the first time in all of their nakedness, and, for the first time, felt ashamed. That shame caused them to hide from God and make fig leaves to cover their "newfound" nakedness. This reveals that, among other things, sin also makes us stupid — thinking you can hide from the creator of the universe! Recently, there was a perfect example in the newspaper of the delusion that sin causes:

Man Blames Cat for Child Porn Downloads

Florida investigators say a man accused of downloading child pornography is blaming his cat. Keith _____ of Jensen Beach is charged with 10 counts of possession of child pornography after detectives found more than 1,000 images on his home computer.

According to a sheriff's report yesterday, Griffin told investigators that his cat jumped on the computer keyboard while he was downloading music. He said he had left the room and found 'strange things' on his computer when he returned.[8]

Throughout the history of mankind, people have continued sinning like Adam and Eve and continued attempting to hide from God, fearing that if he ever saw them in all their naked ugliness, he would reject them. This desire to hide from God led to the invention of religion, which is found in some form in every culture. As Christians, one of the primary places we have learned to hide from God is in the church. More people are hiding from God behind their fig leaves on Sundays than any other time. In fact, there's often more honesty to be found at the local pub.

Many years ago Kim and I went to a pastor's conference at a Baptist church in Florida led by Pastor Peter Lord. Peter was a wonderful example of a leader who was not afraid to show his uglies. He taught one session on the "Danger of Wearing Masks" and he used the words of Jesus from Luke 12:1-3, warning his followers about the "leaven of the Pharisees," which meant hypocrisy. He described how leaven worked in making bread —

8. Alex Leo, "Man Blames Cat For Child Porn Downloads," The Huffington Post, http://www.huffingtonpost.com/2009/08/13/man-blames-cat-for-child-_n_258752.html (accessed September 11, 2010). This proves my point that sin makes us stupid and confirms my suspicion that cats are evil!

adding just a tiny amount would cause the entire loaf to rise; and so it is with wearing religious masks. Pretending is a spiritual disease that can quickly spread throughout the entirety of our spiritual lives. The word Jesus used for hypocrisy is the word used for the masks that actors of his time would hold over their faces to represent different characters in their dramas.

After being warned of the danger of wearing masks, Pastor Lord sent us out to gather in small groups of four or five pastors to practice removing our masks — exposing our uglies and then taking time to minister to each other. This is how church is supposed to work! I was twenty-four and the youngest in my group by about twenty years. I could not wait to receive the wisdom from these great men of God. One of the older ones started out attempting to take off his mask by exposing some impatience he had with his wife and children. I thought about how great it would be to one day be so holy that my biggest struggle was being a little impatient. That was not even on my first page of sins!

I was next, and off came the mask. I shared about struggling with lust, pornography, and masturbation; which was something that I had never shared with anyone before. The look of shock said it all! You would have thought I shared about being an ax-murderer or a child molester. I unknowingly broke the secret religious code of pastors (which is, among other things, to never tell the whole truth about yourself), and now I was vulnerable. Here I was, years past high school, still hitting sprinkler heads and lying naked before my peers. Except this time, instead of my manhood being attacked, I felt my spirituality was being questioned as the pastors ministered to me like I was the "ugly duckling" who had become the group project. I really appreciated all of their concern, prayers and wise counsel, but I would have experienced a much deeper healing if they could have had the spiritual *cajones*[9] to remove their own masks, and shared the truths of their own sexual sins. It has been said that there are two main sins men struggle with, one is sexual temptation and the other is lying about sexual temptation.[10]

So there I was, lying naked before my peers with nothing but ugly showing. They didn't cover me with the beauty of the grace that they had experienced, only with spiritual sounding words and cold prayers. Limping away from that group of pastors, I had flashbacks to my high school streaking experience. The only difference was that I did not tell the pastors to f*** off (but I sure was thinking it).

I was Ugly Jamie that day, but I discovered the beauty of God's grace as I took off my mask. The other pastors preserved their appearance of dignity as the holy men of God — pretty pastors who could be admired, as strong, together, and good-looking — but inside they suffered, unhealed, still playing the hiding game with God. These pastors remained covered only by their own religious fig leaves, and missed the beauty of his grace that covers our weaknesses.

I know there are many "rational" explanations for why a lot of religious leaders learn to wear masks (such as painful experiences caused by mean, religious people). Being a pastor for over thirty years, I have often felt the condemning stares of critical, hyper-religious people. My family has been judged in every way you

---

9. For those of you from Ohio, *cajones* are "testicles."

10. And, by the way, after these pastors worked me over "in love," the next pastor confessed a dark secret sin of speeding! I long for the day when at the top of the list of sins I'm struggling with is driving too fast. What a joy it would be to fall on my knees and cry out to God for mercy because I was slipping back into speeding. My reality is struggling with giving the finger to some wacko from Canada as I speed around them. One of my favorite preachers, Charles Swindoll, says, "Your right foot is the last part of your body to get saved." For some of us, we need to add in the middle finger as well.

could imagine. People see your ugly places and then exploit them — just like tabloids do to famous people with ugly butts — somehow feeling more righteous in the process of judging others. After awhile, you learn to hide your ugliness to save yourself the pain. But this poison is a far greater danger to our hearts than the wounds inflicted by critical, self-righteous judgments.[11]

I want a spirituality that the late Mike Yaconelli speaks of so refreshingly in his book, *Messy Spirituality*. Yaconelli unveils the myth of flawlessness and summons Christians everywhere to "come out of hiding and stop pretending."[12] Later, at the retreat with Peter Lord, one of the pastors approached me and shared that he was having some of the same struggles that I had shared about. We then cried together and prayed for one another. We covered each other's nakedness, not with denial and masks, but with grace. There is a story in the Bible in the ninth chapter of Genesis that illustrates this principle of *being* covered with grace. Noah, after surviving the flood, overdid it in celebrating one night and was found naked in his tent, passed out from his drunkenness. One of his sons, Ham, walked in and stared at his nakedness. He then ran

---

11. One time I was ministering from my weaknesses (see *Ugly Preaching*, Chapter 12), sharing about some struggles I was having with fear. I was just being Ugly Jamie. The next week I had an appointment with a couple that announced they were leaving the church. When I inquired as to why, they said they "did not want a doubting pastor who struggled with fear," and quoted 2 Timothy 1:7 (KJV) to me: "for God hath not given us the spirit of fear." I asked them if they would prefer a pastor who was a liar? (I know many pastors and all of them struggle with something; especially fear.) Surprisingly, they found no humor in my question, and off they went to discover a pretty pastor who was better at masking his ugly than I was. Many people choose to just watch churches on TV that have pastors who are always scripted, edited, and wearing plenty of physical and religious makeup. You will never catch one of them picking their nose!

12. Michael Yaconelli, *Messy Spirituality* (Grand Rapids, MI: Zondervan Publishing Co., 2007), 24.

out and began reporting the news to others.[13] When they heard of their father's "fall," the other sons refused to look at his nakedness and shame; instead, they "... walked backward and covered their father's nakedness" (Gen 9:23). This walking backwards needs to become a spiritual discipline in the church. We need to have "Backward Walk of Grace" classes taught in our seminaries. Maybe by doing this, we can save some believers and pastors from hiding their sins and falling into the evil one's traps.

I will gladly drop my stones of self-righteous condemnation, take off my mask, and fall naked at the feet of Jesus — joining the woman caught in adultery — just to hear those healing words of grace "... neither do I condemn you" (John 8:11). What great joy to lift my head without shame, look into the forgiving, loving eyes of God, and see a huge smile on his face. Because of that, I will continue to just be Ugly Jamie. And because of that, I will continue to be covered by the beauty of God's Grace. Is that a rock in your hand?

Remember the words from the classic hymn, *Rock of Ages*:

> Nothing in my hand I bring,
> Simply to the cross I cling;
> Naked, come to Thee for dress;
> Helpless, look to Thee for grace;
> Foul, I to the fountain fly;
> Wash me, Savior, or I die[14]

---

13. In the culture of that day, it was a great shame for a male to be seen naked — and it was extremely disrespectful for someone to look at another person's nakedness. Honoring your parents, especially fathers, was also a very sacred duty in their culture.

14. Music by Augustus M. Toplady and Words by Thomas Hastings, *Rock of Ages* (Public Domain).

There are triumphant defeats that rival victories.
— Os Guinness

Chapter 3. Ugly Winning

I Pick Randy

When you listen to athletes giving interviews after their victories, they often thank God for how well they did. They may say something like, "I just want to give God all of the glory." What I have never seen in all my years of watching sports is a player from a losing team say, "I want to thank God for helping us play such a terrible game today and causing us to suffer such an ugly defeat. I give him all the glory for this humiliating loss." I've never seen it because in America, we worship at the altar of success. As famous football coach Vince Lombardi once said, "Winning isn't everything, it is the only thing."[1] This drive for success — to be bigger, faster, and stronger at whatever cost — leads to many evils in our society. The sad thing is that this is the mindset of many in the church also, even the leaders.

I have been infected all my life with the drive to win. It is a disease that tells me I have to be the best or else I am a total failure. But every so often, maybe because of my inherent stubbornness, I choose to resist it.

In Mrs. Hyde's fifth grade class, when we had recess, we usually played a game called Greek Dodge Ball. I have no idea why we called it that, but the rules were simple. There were two teams, two

---

1. David Maraniss, *When Pride Still Mattered: A Life Of Vince Lombardi* (New York, NY: Simon & Schuster, 2000).

balls, and three ropes. Each team would take their side. We had to throw the ball at the opposing players and try to hit them and get them out. If we threw the ball and they caught it, we were out.[2] The way that we picked teams was simple, too; the teacher would have two of the best players take turns selecting their teammates. It was a lot like the NFL draft, just without the millions of dollars. One day it was Greg against me (as usual). We had a fierce rivalry over who would lead the class; we were like two young lions trying to prove to the others that we were the toughest, strongest, and the best at everything.[3]

So every day we picked teams the same way. I picked David, Greg picked Billy, and on and on until we got to the weaklings and the losers that no one wanted on their teams. Usually it was girls, yet there were some like Donna who was better than most boys. How traumatic it must have been to be a boy and to be picked last. What rejection and humiliation! Kids are so mean. They see weakness (ugliness), and they tease, mock, and make fun of every imperfection. Many children wear scars left from mean words into adulthood.[4] It doesn't really get easier as we get older; the stakes just go up.

This makes me think of a friend of mine who had a crush on this really pretty popular girl.[5] They were at the school dance

---

2. I'm sure you care all about learning how to play Greek Dodge Ball, but I'll spare you all of the details! And I know, it probably just sounds a lot like Dodge Ball.

3. Truth be told, I was afraid of Greg — he was stronger than I. But, I was more afraid of failing, so I never showed any weakness.

4. I'm convinced that some of these children never deal with their pain — they just grow up to be photographers for the tabloids. They spend their adult lives making a living by pointing out the failures and weaknesses of others. "Look whose fat butt this is!"

5. I'm not sure why guys set themselves up for rejection by aiming too

and he finally worked up the nerve to walk over and ask her to dance. This is one of the longest most difficult walks across a room a high school male will ever make. As he walked up to ask for the next dance, unbeknownst to him, he blew a snot bubble out of one of his nostrils (he had recurring sinus problems). That snot bubble was just hanging there as he — in the most sexy way possible — said "Hey, babe. You want to take a walk on the wild side with me? Let's dance!" She took one look at that bubble and gagged as she said, "Gross! How immature!" (She thought he had done it on purpose.) She spun around and huffed as she walked away. Meanwhile, all of the girls were just laughing at my poor, rejected, bubble-nose friend.[6]

As a fifth grader, I had no faith in God, and my family rarely went to church. I have no explanation for what happened one particular day in Mrs. Hyde's class — it could be that I was so prideful and cocky that I thought that I could win no matter what. But I want to believe that it was the grace of God working in my life; planting seeds of kingdom leadership that one day would bear fruit in an ugly pastor who leads an ugly church that is filled with the beauty of God.

"I pick Randy!"

A hush fell over the class, and no one moved, especially Randy. You see Randy was born with a deformed hand that was missing the three fingers between the thumb and pinky. There were just little nubs where there should have been fingers. Randy was small and frail. He was always chosen last, with some painful comment thrown in like, "Ha-ha! You got stuck with Randy!"

---

far over their heads for a date, but we do it a lot. I think it's because the country music singer Lyle Lovett gave every ugly boy in the country hope when he married Julia Roberts.

6. I have always secretly hoped that she grew up to be that pretty girl who was picking her booger on Monday Night Football.

I'm sure he hated school. With the class still in shock and before I could change my mind Greg blurted out, "I pick David." As Randy made his way to the front of the class as astonished as everyone else, I made my next selection, "I pick Sally." Sally was a tall girl with crooked teeth. Her hair was never combed, and she smelled.[7] We never showed her any mercy. No one even wanted to hold hands with her when we made circles — we thought we might get cooties. God forgive me for having such a hard heart.

But this day was different. Greg shouted, "I get Billy!" and the class began to laugh at how stupid I was being. I went down the list, picking everybody who was usually picked last while Greg continued picking the strongest and fastest. Out to recess we went, with the other team mocking. "We're going to cream you! Stilson, you're an idiot to pick all those losers!"

My team huddled around me as though I could offer them some protection from the evil ones taunting them. What had I done? Was this going to be a David and Goliath story? Was this going to be the *Miracle on Dirt?* Were the headlines going to read *Underdogs Win?*

How great it would make this story if that had happened. It would be a glorious sacrifice on the altar of winning. I could stand before the press and give God all the glory for helping us win, knowing deep down it was really because of my superior abilities. The ugly reality is that it was not even close — we were crushed, over and over. I was humiliated! Why did I do such a stupid thing? Was I that arrogant? Looking back, so many years later, the experience has been filled with rich meaning.

---

7. I grew up in an upper middle class family and was never exposed to poverty. I have so much guilt over how ignorant and arrogant I was back then. I would hate to know what kind of home she had lived in, but kids never stop to ask these questions.

Without knowing it, I acted more like God than I could ever have imagined. I modeled how God picks his team! God would make a terrible NFL owner or coach. His team would lose every game! God's kingdom operates by a different set of rules than this world does. Success in God's kingdom often involves terrible defeat in the eyes of the world, and the cross is the best example of this. What appeared to be a complete failure, turned out, by God's power, to be the greatest triumph in history. In God's kingdom, a terrible loss can be radically transformed into a powerful win — it is Ugly Winning. "Jesus' cross suggests that, 'mission can not be realized when we are powerful and confident but only when we are weak and at a loss.'"[8]

God uses the cross to confuse those who think that they are wise and trust in their own strength (1 Cor 1:18). The cross is the best thing "to confound people who build their confidence and their whole life on a distorted understanding of power and wisdom...the Cross defines power in the kingdom as powerlessness."[9] Powerlessness is essentially an act of faith. In our powerlessness we express our dependence on God.

That day in Mrs. Hyde's fifth grade class, the kingdom of God was present. I was completely unaware of it, but I was acting like Jesus. I chose my team as if they were valuable — not because they were strong, powerful, and needed. I chose to love and value them in spite of their ugliness. Winning was not found in defeating Greg's superior team; it was showing mercy to those who had never known it. Of course, there are huge differences

---

8. Jayakuma Christian, *God of the Empty-Handed: Poverty, Power & the Kingdom of God* (Monrovia, CA: World Vision International, 1999), 199. Quoted by David J Bosch.

9. Ibid. He goes on to write that "By refusing to play the power game with the powerful, the Christian makes a political statement. Kingdom power proclaims the sovereignty of Jesus' way over against the powers of this age."

between Jesus and myself! He picks ugly people and then reveals his beauty through them. He picks the weak "nobodies" who know that anything good that happens in their lives is always the grace of God. These people truly can give God all the glory for their victories.

* * *

Why is it so hard for Christians to understand the way God picks his team? Throughout the Bible, God chooses ugly people to accomplish his purposes. He shows us that we are not disqualified from serving on his team because of our weaknesses. It is our beauty, our strengths, that hinder us — we are too strong to fully depend on him, too smart to seek his wisdom, and too important to do the crappy jobs.

I've always wanted a strong church that could make me look good and cover up all of my inadequacies, but in reality God surrounds me with a team made up of Randys and Sallys. I must confess that more than once I have complained to God about the group of people he has called me to lead. "But Lord, they are so weak and needy, many of them are unemployed, many of them have addictions or marriage issues. They are all so draining. How are we going to make a difference in this world; let alone pay the bills?" The Lord answered one of these prayers (or, to put it more honestly, complaining sessions) by reminding me of a wonderful story of how he picks a winning team from rejects.

The story is found in the life of David in 1 Samuel 22. David was on the run, being hunted like an animal by the king, Saul. Saul was filled with rage and jealousy toward David and wanted to kill him because God had chosen David to take his place as king over Israel. David, at this low point in his life, ended up hiding in a cave called Adullam. Since David had no army to lead, God began to pick David's team for him. I find it funny that at no point did God ask for David's input. The Bible says, "... every one that was in distress, and every one that was in debt, and every one that was discontented, gathered themselves unto [David]; and he became a captain over them" (1 Sam 22:2, KJV).

What an ugly bunch of rejects! God reached down into the bottom of the barrel and dragged out a group of losers. There were four hundred of them, and they became King David's army. You may have heard of the Dirty Dozen, well this was the Filthy Four Hundred. It was filled with Randys and Sallys and Jamies — ugly people who were drawn to a weak, broken king because he was just like them. God took this flawed team and turned it into a mighty army that succeeded in bringing the whole nation together to follow David. Guess who gets the credit when an army like that wins? I will let King David tell you in his own words, "Through God we shall do valiantly: for he it is that shall tread down our enemies" (Ps 60:12, KJV).

*　*　*

Have you ever wondered why most rock stars end up going down the same path? Just watch VH1 and they'll tell you where yesterday's rock stars are today. They all follow a similar pattern — they hit it big; sell a million albums; and then get lots of women, money, and addictions. There is a tragedy, overdose, crash, arrest, or divorce, and then the band breaks up. Some come to Jesus and change a few words in a song to make it "Christian." Why don't you ever see someone coming to Jesus when they are at the top? In a word: Pride. Who needs Jesus when everything is going great? Why would you need God when you have everything you ever dreamed about? This is the danger of the Ugly Beauty that is man's boast without God. What we can accomplish on our own, and for our own glory, is evil in the sight of God.[10]

It was no different for me, except I was never a rock star. I came to Jesus through the crushing defeat of being arrested for drugs. It was in my despair that I cried out to Jesus. I had to be humbled. As long as we have thoughts like "God should pick me for his team, because I will help him win," or "God needs what I bring to the team," we will continue to be overlooked. He does not need anything I have to offer him, but I need everything that he has to offer me.

God is courageous (some would even say foolish) to risk all of his kingdom on ugly people like me. Oswald Chambers captures God's style of Ugly Winning while commenting on Luke 18:31, "Then he took unto him the twelve:"

> The bravery of God in trusting us! You say — 'But He has been unwise to choose me, because there is nothing in me; I am not of any value.' That is why He chose you. As long as you think there is something in you, He cannot choose you because you have ends of your own to serve; but if you have let him bring you to the end of your self-sufficiency then He can choose you to go with Him…"[11]

God loves to make the world scratch its head. Even the angels are confused about the mysterious ways of God's picking his team (1 Pet 1:12). I can almost hear the shock in the hallways of heaven, much like the ones in Mrs. Hyde's fifth grade class, as God announces his first-round selection in the Salvation Draft — "I pick Jamie." How could he pick such a rebellious loser? There's no way God will win at anything if he keeps making picks like that.

His team is made of weak nobodies who have nothing to offer,

---

10. Isaiah 64:6 says, "All of us have become like one who is unclean, and all our righteous acts are like filthy rags…" Have you ever asked God to forgive you for your goodness?

11. Oswald Chambers, *My Utmost for His Highest* (New York, NY: Dodd, Mead, and Company, 1935), 217.

but are completely dependent on him. Their only boast is in him, so he receives all the glory. The way God picks his team can be seen in this story about Saint Francis.

> One day, as St Francis was returning from the forest, where he had been in prayer, Brother Masseo, wanted to test his humility. The Brother went to him and asked, "Why after you? Why is it that the entire world goes after you? Why do all men wish to see you, hear you, and obey you? You aren't handsome, learned, or of noble birth. Why is it that all the world goes after you?"

> Upon hearing these words, St Francis rejoiced greatly in spirit. He lifted up his eyes to heaven and remained in prayer for a long time. Then he knelt down to the ground and gave thanks to God with great fervor of spirit. He answered Brother Masseo, "You want to know why all men come after me? It is because the Lord who is in heaven and sees the evil and the good in all places has found no one among men that is more wicked, more imperfect, or a greater sinner than I am. To accomplish the wonderful work that he intends to do, he has found no creature more vile on earth than I am. It is for this reason that he has chosen me: to confound all strength, beauty, greatness, noble birth, and all the science of the world. That men may learn that every virtue and every good gift comes from him, and not from any creature. That no one may glory before God; but if any one glory, let him glory in the Lord."[12]

Saint Francis realized that as long as he was relying on God's grace, he didn't need to ask "why me?" Instead, because he knew the wonder of God's grace, he could boldly proclaim, "Why not me?"

Can you stop for a moment to get real still so you can listen? God is still picking his team; will you hear him calling your name? Do not let the noise of your fears, or the accusing voice of "why you," drown out his call of grace. Remember,

---

12. St. Francis of Assisi, *Little Flowers of St Francis* (Public Domain). This story is adapted from Chapter 10 where Saint Francis is elaborating on 1 Corinthians 1:27-29.

it's not about you and your abilities or strengths; it's about God picking weak, ugly people. Through these people, he can display the beauty of his grace. This is The Power of Ugly, and he always wins, even if it is Ugly Winning.

So why not you?

God's reckless grace is our greatest hope and a life
changing experience.
— Timothy Keller

Chapter 4. Ugly Exchange

Stilson Scores

Growing up I was extremely competitive, and I got bored quickly with sports that I didn't excel in. Eventually, I discovered that I was made for football! At least, in my heart I was...but the rest of my body probably would have been more suited to bowling. I thought that the game was perfect for me; it seemed to me to be more about violence than finesse. I was not fast, big, or very strong — all of which are required for any good football player. I made up for these shortcomings by being passionate, committed, and reckless.[1]

I found my place at middle linebacker, just like my hero from the Chicago Bears, number 51, Dick Butkus.[2] I had the honor to play for four years wearing number 51 for the Fort Myers High School "Green Wave" football team. We were called the "Greenies," which, looking back, does not sound very intimidating, but we thought we were. We were led by a legend in high school football, Coach Sam Sirianni — whom we respectfully called Coach Sam. He was the only authority figure that I respected in

---

1. These are all just nice ways of saying that I was mean!

2. With a name like that, you had no choice but to be tough! One of the toughest kids I knew in school was named "Harry Butts." What were his parents smoking? It was worse than a "Boy Named Sue." Let me tell you, though, no one dared to make fun of Harry — to his face at least!

my rebellious teen years.[3]

We always did pranks in the locker room before practice. Once, we found a condom in a kid named Rick's locker. We filled it with water, tied it to his helmet, and put it in the freezer overnight. It was a blast watching him attempt to put his helmet on the next day with the large frozen item hanging out of it! Another good one was the masterpiece of leaving a nasty deposit in someone's helmet overnight instead of flushing that deposit down the toilet. When the coach blew the whistle for practice to begin, we watched with great delight as the kid pulled his helmet on only to discover the "blessing" that had been left for him![4]

My most painfully favorite prank was lighting an M-80 (which is about one-tenth of a stick of dynamite) and placing it under a trashcan in the locker room. We ran out of the locker room, but failed to warn the few underclassmen that were dressing by the can (and, of course, the coaches). It went off like a sonic boom, catapulting the can to the ceiling. As the smoke billowed through the locker room, Coach Sam came out swearing, "Who is the [blankety blank] that set off that [blankety blank blank] explosive?" Of course, under fear of reprisal, the team was silent. I was one of the captains and no one would dare rat me out.

Our team manager, Carl, was a little slow — he was not the sharpest knife in the drawer.[5] He came running out of the smoke-filled locker room shouting, "Coach Sam, Coach Sam! I know who

---

3. This is one of the reasons that I am so passionate about seeing kids get involved in sports, even with all the excesses of competition and risk of injury. A good coach can fulfill a father roll; and at times, he is even like a pastor.

4. I still laugh out loud as I am writing this; is that wrong?

5. After high school, Carl continued faithfully assisting Coach Sam by holding the wire from his headset during the games to keep it from getting tripped over. Carl did this for over twenty years until Coach Sam died.

did it!" Carl spoke very nasally in a high pitch, "but I cannot tell you his name." I relaxed and stopped planning how I would kill him. But then he said, "I can't tell you his name," and I believe he meant that with all sincerity, "but his initials are 'Jamie Stilson.'" I knew I was dead. After practice that day, I ran laps in full pads in the hot and humid Florida sunshine until I barfed. Meanwhile, the whole team watched and cheered from the bleachers.[6]

Carl made up for turning me in when we were on our graduating class trip to Disney World. I took way too many drugs that day and got myself lost in Fort Wilderness. All my friends blew me off because I was acting so weird, but Carl found me. He said, "Jamie don't worry, I know the way out of here." It was like being led around Disney World by Forrest Gump. Carl could not find the way out of Fort Wilderness either, so we spent five hours together wandering around and looking for the exit. It was the blind leading the blind. He was an ugly companion, but he proved that he was more faithful than my pretty friends were; he stuck with me in spite of me.[7]

Everyone needs a Carl in their life. We need to have someone who doesn't think we're any kind of big deal, someone who is not afraid of us. We need someone who always tells the truth, even if it is more than they meant to say. Someone who helps us find our way when we are lost. Someone who is not ashamed to be with us, even when we are behaving like drugged-out idiots. Carl was acting more like Jesus than most Christians I know. I hope when I grow up, I will be like Carl. He may be ugly, but he is beautiful to Jesus and to me. Do you have any Carls in your life? If not, I

---

6. You probably want to ask me if it was worth it? Absolutely!

7. I never thanked you, Carl, for being Jesus' hands and feet (but not eyes). So, thanks for being a friend that "sticks closer than a brother." Thanks for helping me escape from Fort Wilderness!

would ask Jesus to send some your way.[8]

Thirty years later I was mowing my lawn when the Lord surprised me with his still small voice.[9] I know hearing voices sounds like flashbacks from my old acid days, but I have learned to pay attention to these impressions that come from Jesus.[10] As I cut the grass, I had the impression, "Coach Sam is dying and you will take part in his memorial." My heart sank and my eyes filled with tears. I knew he was battling cancer, but I did not know that it was that far along. At that moment, God reminded me of a story from my past that he wanted me to share at his memorial. After that, I was able to spend some quality time with Coach Sam in the hospital. We shared old stories like the M-80, and laughed. What an honor it was to share faith together and to pray for Coach Sam. He had found a personal relationship with Jesus through his cancer.[11]

---

8. I think we should make a W.W.C.D. bracelet — asking the question "What Would Carl Do?" This is probably better than asking "What Would Jesus Do?" The problem with asking W.W.J.D. is that nobody knows! Jesus is full of surprises, and just when you think you have him figured out, he goes and blows your mind. The second problem with W.W.J.D. is best illustrated by the story a local police officer told me of discovering two teens in the back of a car making out — naked except for their W.W.J.D. bracelets. Knowing what Jesus would do, and having the power to do it are two different things. Maybe we can start with W.W.C.D. and work our way up to W.W.J.D.!

9. But his voice sure can be loud sometimes too!

10. Sometimes you need to test your impressions with someone you trust that has a relationship with Jesus. When what you hear is about a serious life changing direction, don't be afraid to ask others for their input. We will talk more about this in *Ugly Mystic*. See Chapter 11. Now, when you receive an impression that says, "Jamie, you need to do the dishes for Kim," you know that it is from the devil!

11. One time in the hospital, I had to become a linebacker again for the Coach. I was in the hospital room with him when a Bible thumping whacko burst in "on a mission from God!" He said, "Jesus has sent me to heal the Coach!" Then he pronounced "in Jesus' name you are healed Coach Sam!" He

The night Coach Sam died there was a Green Wave football home game (in what is now called the Sam Sirianni Stadium). Many folks wanted to cancel the game, but his lovely wife Margaret, who never missed a game in Coach Sam's thirty-three years of coaching, said, "Sam would want them to play." His son Sammy (who was the ball boy when I played) was now the head coach. I was asked to announce the passing of Coach Sam and give the invocation. Carl was there, too, now holding the cord for Coach Sammy, but the stadium seemed empty without Coach Sam at the sidelines. They won that night, but the victory seemed empty after such a loss. Death has a way of putting things into perspective and helping us put our priorities in order. Death redefines what winning and losing mean.

The memorial for Coach Sam filled the stadium with thousands of people. There were former players, now in the NFL, other coaches, friends, and family taking part in the memorial. I had been given three minutes to speak — and of course, I went a little over. I was sitting on the platform with a couple of other ministers with whom the family had asked me to coordinate the spiritual part of the service. One of the pastors that I was asked to invite to take part proved to be a difficult assignment for me. He was fairly new in town and was the pastor of one of the largest churches. The former pastor of his church had ordained me into the ministry. I had tried to reach out to this pastor several times only to be snubbed by him. He was such a big shot and I was just a pastor of a small, ugly church. But I pressed through my

---

told the Coach to just "claim it, and it was done." Now I believe in healing "in Jesus name," and we had been praying for that. However, this guy had no compassion, wisdom, or sensitivity; just "faith." He may have heard voices, but he should have sought out some wise counsel. How many people have been assaulted in the name of faith? I "lovingly" escorted him out the door "in Jesus' name." On his way out, I noticed that he might have been wearing a W. W .J. D. bracelet!

pride — which involved addressing him as "Pastor" or "Doctor" so-and-so at his insistence. I bit my tongue,[12] called him "Pastor," (with blood dripping out of both sides of my mouth) and invited him to participate in the memorial.

When it came time for me to share, I told this story:

> I played for Coach Sam in the '70s, and my senior year I was one of the team captains. For one of our out of town games, my good friend Nicky Powell and I came up with a plan (my idea of course) to do something different. Nicky was one of the best players to ever play for Coach Sam. He was a wide receiver who scored most of our touchdowns. Nicky wore number 17, which happened to be my favorite number. I wore number 51 because you could not play my position and wear number 17.[13]
>
> I played football for a total of 8 seasons, playing in over 70 games and in all of those games I had never scored a touchdown.[14] But that night was going to be different! I came up with this great idea to exchange jerseys with Nicky. Of course we did not ask for permission. In those days football players did not wear their names on the back of their jerseys, so your number was your identity. The announcers just went by the numbers on the roster to identify the player. When Nicky and I traded jerseys he became "number fifty-one, Stilson" and I became "number seventeen, Powell." We had exchanged identities!
>
> I played a very forgetful game that night; in fact, it was downright ugly. I missed several key tackles and got in a fight

---

12. And I looked at my W.W.C.D. bracelet.

13. Watch for the number 17 throughout this book as it serves as fingerprints of God reminding me that he is in charge of every step of my life. I later discovered that I really did wear number 17, because 51 is 17 times 3.

14. The closest that I ever came to scoring a touchdown was recovering a fumble on the one-yard line. I heard footsteps, and in fear, lunged on top of the ball instead of picking it up and taking one step to score. When I looked up, I realized that those footsteps were all of my teammates surrounding me. They looked down at me lying on the ball and said, "Stilson you idiot, why didn't you just fall into the end zone and score?" This is a good example of how fear can rob you.

resulting in a 15-yard penalty and almost being ejected from the game — but the announcers always called out "number seventeen, Powell, is being penalized for unsportsmanlike conduct." It wasn't a game that would make a mother proud — the only times "number seventeen" was called that night it involved something bad. You could say that "number seventeen, Powell," played a terrible game.

On the other hand, Nicky, wearing my jersey, had a fantastic game — all night over the loudspeakers you could hear, "Number fifty-one, Stilson on the reception; Stilson scores!" Three times that night it was announced, "Number fifty-one, Stilson, scores!" I couldn't believe it. My name was being celebrated for scoring a touchdown. It felt weird, and it felt wrong, but I loved it! It was the greatest game I had *ever played;* yet it was the greatest game that I *never played.*

We had made an exchange of identities. Nicky suffered and Jamie triumphed. Nicky's victories became mine and my defeats became his — not a fair exchange. It turned out to be an Ugly Exchange for Nicky, but a beautiful exchange for Jamie. After the game, we received a butt chewing from Coach Sam for the switch up. I also got one for all my penalties.[15]

Coach Sam was a wonderful man, but like all of us, he had his weaknesses and sins. I stand here tonight with great confidence that Coach Sam is with Jesus in heaven, not because he was perfect but because he made an Ugly Exchange. Coach Sam traded his sins for Jesus' righteousness. When Coach Sam placed his faith in Jesus, he traded jerseys with Jesus — in a spiritual sense. When Jesus died on the cross, he took Coach Sam's sins on himself, and in exchange, he gave Coach Sam his forgiveness and grace. Coach Sam entered heaven by exchanging lives with Jesus.

Every one of the other thirty-plus speakers received applause after their talks. It was completely silent after mine. God's presence had entered the stadium as the Good News of Jesus was shared. "The world thirsts for grace. When grace descends, the world falls

---

15. Coach Sam found no humor from me suggesting that it was Powell who got those penalties, not me.

silent before it."[16] My wife, sitting with the dignitaries and other speakers, overheard one saying, "What does this guy think, that this is some kind of a church service?" Yes, I did.

As I sat down, fearing that I had overdone it, the pastor that had snubbed me several times patted my knee and paid me one of the best and most timely compliments I have ever received. "You just scored your touchdown," he said. These words were life to me and overcame all my hurt feelings towards him. I never thanked him either! Pastor, thank you for being the mouth of Jesus to me and speaking those words of encouragement.[17]

* * *

The Apostle Paul shares about this amazing, unfair, and ugly exchange with these words found in 2 Corinthians 5:21 (KJV). "For [God] has made [Jesus] to be sin for us, who knew no sin; that we might be made the righteousness of God in him [Jesus]."

This is the greatest Ugly Exchange that anyone can ever make. Whose jersey are you wearing? You can't wear two jerseys; there's only one number per player. Letting go of fifty-one in exchange for seventeen was easy. I gave up my ugliness for his touchdowns. When I walked forward in a Baptist church as an eighteen-year-old broken drug addict who was completely lost and wandering around in the Fort Wilderness of this world, I made the greatest Ugly Exchange in my life. As the congregation sang, "Just as I am without one plea, but that thy blood was shed for me," I fell to my knees in surrender. I gave Jesus my sins, pain, emptiness, meanness, and all of the ugliness of Jamie in exchange for the beauty of his grace, mercy, forgiveness, and righteousness. I found

16. Philip Yancey, *What's So Amazing About Grace?* (Grand Rapids, MI: Zondervan Publishing Co., 1997), 282.

17. I think I noticed that he was now wearing a W. W. C. D. bracelet.

a new peace, the Holy Spirit, and eternal life as I made Jesus the Lord of my life.

Wow, does he lose in this Ugly Exchange! Yet that is the miracle of God's love; he thinks that we are worth it. The value God places in ugly people like me can be best explained through the words of the song written by a former slave trader, John Newton, who made the Ugly Exchange; "Amazing Grace how sweet the sound that saved a wretch like me. I once was lost but now I am found was blind but now I see." Have you made this Ugly Exchange? It will cost you giving up your "number" — your accomplishments, your goodness, and your selfish, independent life of you being your own boss — and surrendering to Jesus as the Lord of your life. You must accept his sacrifice for you on the cross as the payment for all your sin. Open your heart and invite Jesus to come and be your Lord.

Thank you, Jesus, for being willing to trade places with us on the cross and making the Ugly Exchange with us!

There is, even in the poorest and crudest prayer,
a touch of Pentecost.
— Henri Bremond, a Jesuit Priest 1865-1933

Chapter 5. Ugly Prayer

The Magic Mushroom

Geoff was one of my best friends all through high school. We did everything together. A group of our friends made a pact in ninth grade to shave our heads like Kung Fu for football our senior year; but out of all of us, Geoff loved his hair the most.[1] At the start of our senior year, I showed up to practice sporting a bald head and a ten-inch ponytail. Geoff had just had his hair trimmed so he would look like Jim Morrison from the Doors. He called me dirty words and went off to have his head shaved.

Geoff was also there the night that a group of our friends were camping in the woods.[2] We were all drinking and doing drugs, trying to find out the meaning of life, when someone started talking about God. With all the great wisdom of a sixteen-year-old hippie (who was drugged out of his mind) I blurted, "There is no God!" Just to overstate the point I stood up, shook my fist, and said, "If there is a God out there, let

---

1. There were seven of us who took the vow.

2. We called the spot where we were camping, "Camp Newt." It was named after one of my good friends who was with us that night — Kevin Rich. While I was writing this book, Kevin passed away and I performed his memorial. Knowing that he joined Geoff, who had already passed away, in heaven gives me great joy.

him..." (I was going to say strike me down with lightning, but some faint little voice of reason deep inside of me said, "You better not say that just to be safe," so I redirected my challenge). "If there is a God let him strike this tree down with lightning!"[3]

As the words left my drunken mouth, all my friends turned, looking to the sky and awaiting God's response. Meanwhile, I passed out and began throwing up. I was choking on my own vomit and probably would have died if Geoff hadn't rolled me over on my stomach so that I could cough out everything I was gagging on (and probably some of my arrogant pride as well). There I lay in all my great atheistic wisdom and puke.[4] God, in his great mercy, used Geoff to save my life that night, knowing that several years later he would use me to save Geoff's.

After high school, Geoff went to California to work in the film industry and I went to forestry school in Lake City, Florida. I had started selling drugs in high school, and continued to do so in college. Everything in my life changed the day the police showed up at my college dorm room with a warrant for my arrest. There had been an undercover sting operation in my hometown that resulted in the arrest of 180 people, and I happened to be one of them. I spent my first night in prison at the Lake City Jail, and I have never been so afraid in all my life.[5] The worst thing I had to do was to make that dreaded phone call — the call to my parents.

---

3. I sounded a little like the wounded, bitter, Vietnam veteran, Lieutenant Dan in *Forrest Gump* as he challenged God while strapped to the mast of a shrimp boat in the middle of a hurricane. "You call this a storm?"

4. "The fool says in his heart, 'There is no God.'" (Ps 14:1)

5. The Lake City Jail, to say the least, was a crap hole. I was eighteen and I was locked in with about a dozen hardened, grown men who were, in my mind, all named Bubba!

The drug arrest was a big deal in my small hometown and it had been all over the news. They only listed two names on the news report, and mine was one of them. My Dad was a prominent general contractor in town, so his son being arrested was big news. I knew I had brought shame on the family and broken their hearts. The deputy sheriff transported me back home to Fort Myers, where I was put in the Lee County jail.

My father was a big, tough, man's man — whom I both loved and feared. The thought of him getting me out of jail for a drug arrest terrified me. When he bailed me out, he did something I never expected and had never seen him do before. Dad put his big arm around me, with tears in his eyes, and asked me, "Why?" I had no answer for him. The only word that described my life at that point was "lost." I had no purpose, no direction, and nothing worth giving my life for. I knew I was searching for something. There had to be more to life than sex, drugs, and rock n' roll, so I started reading Eastern mystical books, which often quoted the Bible. This stirred interest in me, so I went out and bought my first Bible. I began to read it at college, while I was still on probation from my drug charges. I still used drugs, but I was no longer just trying to get high; I was trying to connect with the spirit world.[6]

One of our favorite things to do in Lake City, a land filled with green pastures and cows, was to go "brown bagging." In high school, I had discovered "magic mushrooms" that grew out of cow manure.[7] They were free and produced a high very similar to LSD. I actually nearly died from them one night,

---

6. I now believe that there was a great battle going on for my soul that I was unaware of at the time.

7. You would think that we might have gotten the hint that they were bad from the fact they grow out of crap!

but it did not stop me from coming back for more, because I had fallen in love with any kind of psychedelic drug.[8]

One night after eating some "shrooms" (as we called them), I attempted to go into a trance to enter the spirit realm so that I could go back into my "former lives." This was something that I had been reading about doing in some of my mystical books. With my eyes shut as I was trying to meditate, I was startled when an angelic being appeared in my mind's eye with his arms extended and crossed as if he was warning: "Stop. Do not go here. Turn around." I was instantly sobered; with no affect of the drugs, which usually would have kept me high for hours. Someone was warning me to not go down this dark path. This drove me back to the Bible that I had bought, and I just kept on reading every verse 17 that I could find. It was as though God wrote each of these verses just for me.

I wanted to give my life to Jesus, but I felt that I was too evil for him to love. This is one of the best lies of the evil one. If Satan cannot keep us from reaching out to Jesus, then he will throw all our sins in our face, accusing us. He will use shame to try to

---

8. Tom Wolfe, *The Electric Kool-Aid Acid Test* (New York, NY: Bantam Books, 1980). In high school I read this notorious book, which was banned from the school. It is about a group of hippies in the '60s who went on a bus trip around the country as they experimented with LSD. A fellow student, who was concerned for my soul, had given me *Peace with God* written by Billy Graham. In my great wisdom, I tore the cover off that book and used it to replace the cover of *The Electric Kool-Aid Acid Test.* Just the sight of a guy — who everyone knew was always stoned — with a shaved head, a ponytail, a large jeweled earring, and dark glasses, reading a Billy Graham book always created quite a stir in the hallways! "Hey, Stilson! Have you flipped out and become a Jesus freak?" I mockingly responded with "I am learning some really cool stuff in this book; it is blowing my mind!" I thought I was so cool, but the Father in heaven just laughed knowing what was coming. He loves to turn the tables on us. To this day, every time I watch Billy Graham preach and he makes the call for people to receive Jesus, I weep. I'm sorry, Billy, for making fun of your book.

choke out God's love. I discovered the wonderful truth found in John 3:17: "For God did not send his Son into the world to condemn the world, but to save the world through him."[9] God loved Jamie in spite of all my evil. He did not come to condemn me, but to rescue me from all of my sin. Ugly Jamie had made the Ugly Exchange and responded to God's call to become a beautiful child of God.[10]

Throughout this journey, the only person that I communicated with was Geoff in California. I often wrote to him about the struggles and changes going on in my life.[11]

While I was going through all of these things, Geoff had become a cocaine addict and weathered a broken marriage. Eventually he came east to visit me back in Fort Myers. One day he asked me if he could borrow my car. I said sure and threw him the keys to "The Rapture Wagon," which is what I had named my car because there were so many Christian bumper stickers on the back that you couldn't even tell what color the car was. I had bumper stickers that boldly proclaimed:

"God Is In Control"

"Jesus Loves You"

"In Case of Rapture This Car Will Be Unmanned"

"Christians Aren't Perfect, Just Forgiven"

And many more. I was changing the world one bumper sticker at a time!

Later that day Geoff returned, pale-white, saying, "I know God will never forgive me." After assuring him that there is nothing

---

9. This was exactly the verse that I needed to see! Most people stop reading at the most famous verse in the Bible, John 3:16, and they miss the verse after it, which is equally as wonderful.

10. I had finally found "Peace with God!"

11. I would love to find those letters!

that God would not forgive, I was fearful of what Geoff was about to confess. He told me that some old guy pulled out in front of him and almost caused Geoff to hit him. Geoff continued on with the story, saying, "I pulled up beside the guy and launched into a tirade of the dirtiest, foulest cuss words I knew. I followed that by giving him the finger and telling him, to go to hell! Then I whipped around him and slammed on the brakes, to give him a taste of what he had done to me. Then I realized, 'O My God! Jamie has all those stupid Christian bumper stickers on the back of his car!'" We laughed together, hoping that the driver focused on the sticker saying "Christians Aren't Perfect, Just Forgiven."[12]

* * *

After making the Ugly Exchange with Jesus, I soon found myself attending seminary in Jacksonville, Florida. I would pick up hitchhikers around town and attempt to witness to them. On one occasion, the Lord used the hitchhiker to teach me. I picked this rough-looking guy and began to share the good news with him when he shocked me by telling me he once was a pastor! He smelled of cigarettes and booze, so I launched into a tirade (in love) about what a hypocrite he was and an embarrassment to Jesus. He began to weep and agreed with me as he told me about how his wife and three children had been killed in a car accident. It took my breath away to hear this horrible story and to realize how hardhearted I was being by judging him. It is so easy to give others the truth of the Bible and never care enough to hear their story.

---

12. I had the joy of helping Geoff come to faith in Jesus. I got to baptize him and perform his marriage to a beautiful, Godly woman named Nancy. Geoff died a few years later after a courageous fight with the terrible disease ALS, also known as Lou Gehrig's Disease. I miss Geoff and I look forward to laughing together again about the many stories we share, especially his ride in "The Rapture Wagon."

Another time while traveling home from Jacksonville to Fort Myers in "The Rapture Wagon," I prayed, "Lord, use me on this trip to share your love with someone." I felt so spiritual offering this prayer — and I was sincere in asking it. The problem was that I thought I knew how God would answer the prayer; I would pick up a hitchhiker and share my story of the Ugly Exchange that I had made with Jesus.

I think the Father in heaven just laughs over the surprises he knows are coming when he answers our prayers. Simple prayers that we pray as new believers are so passionate and can sound so spiritual, but the answers to them are usually devastating! Prayers like "Lord, whatever it takes, make me more like Jesus," or "Father, give me patience," or "Jesus, I will go wherever you want, even to the ends of the earth."

I prayed all of these prayers and more during the first year that I started following Christ. That was before a wise old saint gave me a warning, "Son, have you ever wondered how the Lord will answer these prayers? The answers do not come to us in our sleep through painless dreams. They come in the form of trials, attacks, temptations, sorrow, disillusionment, broken hearts, losses, storms, and 'The Dark Night of the Soul.'"[13] Fear gripped my heart, and I said that I would just take the prayers back and ask the Lord to forgive my ignorance. But he assured me that it was too late; that God was committed to taking the rest of my life to answers these pretty prayers.[14]

---

13. "The Dark Night of the Soul," sounded terrible even though, at the time, I had no idea what it meant. I have since experienced many of these nights, and they are even more terrible than the name sounds! This concept comes from Saint John of the Cross.

14. The truth is, it does not matter whether you ever pray these prayers or not. When you sign up to follow Jesus and confess him as your Lord, God begins the process of conforming us "to the likeness of his Son" (Rom 8:29).

After driving for a few hours, I still had not found a hitchhiker to pick up, but I knew the Lord would answer me. Then, about halfway home, "The Rapture Wagon" died! I was stranded in nowhere land,[15] so I got out of the car and threw a fit, blaming God for letting my car break down. I even tried laying hands on the car and praying for healing, but no luck.

After a several minutes, I looked up to heaven and told the Father I was sorry for complaining and I offered up a heartless, emotionless, only out of obedience, Ugly Prayer: "Father, you know I don't mean this, but in obedience to your word, I praise you for letting my car break down on this desolate back road. Please help me get home." Putting feet to my prayer (Or should I say hands?) I stuck out my thumb to hitchhike home. I still had not figured out that this was all about God answering my original pretty prayer for the Lord to use me.

My first ride was with a group of pot-smoking hippies. They graciously offered me some weed, which I had to decline, even though it smelled sweet. I had the great opportunity to share my faith story with them and prayed with them before they had to let me out. "Far out, dude. Be cool," were their parting words. After that, I had several more rides and opportunities to tell my story.

It was getting late and I was standing on a barren stretch of Highway US-17[16] outside Zolfo Springs. I was still over an hour from home, so I lifted up another Ugly Prayer.[17] I prayed, "Lord,

---

No matter what it takes, or how long it requires, God is committed to finish the task!

15. Remember, this is way before the days of cell phones.

16. Watch for his fingerprints!

17. By now I had "gotten it" about the Lord turning the tables on how he was going to answer my pretty prayer. And I could hear the laughter coming from Heaven.

I'm tired and I want to get home. Please send me a ride going all the way to Fort Myers; and if it's not too much, make it a cool car." I neglected to ask for a safe driver.

Within moments of this Ugly Prayer, a pimped-out Cadillac El Dorado came roaring to a stop in front of me.[18] When the door opened, a beer can rolled past my feet and smoke poured out, and then a voice from inside invited me to "Hop in."[19] I asked the driver where he was heading, and he replied, "Fort Myers," as we roared away. We hit ninety miles per hour before I could even buckle my seat belt — and he wasn't driving in a straight line! His eyes looked like a Georgia road map, and he introduced himself to me as the owner of the "Magic Mushroom" — which was the first topless bar in Fort Myers. Then he handed me a wooden token that said it was good for a free drink at his bar. Can't you just hear the laughter from heaven?

I introduced myself and told him I was a seminary student who was studying to be a pastor. He quickly told me he had no interest in discussing religion, and I agreed not to; however, he seemed to have no trouble talking about Jesus. I shared my story with him, and before we arrived at my house, I was blessed to lead him in a prayer to receive Jesus. I left him with tears of joy running down his cheeks, as he made the Ugly Exchange.

The prophet Isaiah reminds us: "For as the heavens are higher than the earth, so are my ways higher than your ways, and my thoughts than your thoughts" (Isa 55:9). I'm not sure if God always honors pretty prayers, but I know he listens to weak, raw, honest, desperate, Ugly Prayers.

---

18. It looked like the car in *Back to the Future*.

19. This is one of those moments when you must make a quick decision. I whispered a prayer: "O God, help me!" as I hopped in and sank down into thick sheepskin seat covers.

Here is an Ugly Prayer that I learned from the late John Wimber, who was the founder of the Vineyard Community of Churches. I use it all the time, and recommend memorizing it:

O God, O God, O God, Help!

... [God] will respond to the prayer of the destitute,
he will not despise their plea (Ps 102.17).

Only where graves are, is there Resurrection.
— Nietzsche

Chapter 6. Ugly Death

It's All Bullshit

When I was in eighth grade, a new kid moved into our town and began attending school with us. He bragged about being a black belt in karate and bullied everyone he met. One day, he even wore his karate outfit to school to prove that he was tough. This was around the time when *Kung Fu* was a popular show on TV. *Kung Fu* was about a man called "Grasshopper" who could fight five men and defeat them with his bare hands. Because of this, we were all very intimidated by our own version of the "Karate Kid." He often embarrassed me, calling me names, and pushing me in the hallways. I usually would have stood up to a kid that tried this, but this time I found myself intimidated and afraid. Fear is a terrible taskmaster; it will make a slave of us if we allow it to. I spoke to my dad about this kid and my dad said that I needed to stop running and stand up to him![1] So I made up my mind that I was going to confront him, even if it meant an old fashion butt whuppin' for me.

The next day at school, he pushed by me in the hallway as usual and called me a dirty name. But this time I didn't run. Instead I told him to back off. I was gripped with fear about what would happen next. He came over, got right in my face, and threatened

---

1. I had a real "John Wayne" dad.

to destroy me with his karate skills. Before I had time to think it through, I balled up my fist and punched him in the face as hard as I could. What happened next was not at all what I expected. "The Karate Kid" began to scream like a little girl. "He hit me! He hit me!" he hollered as he ran away holding his bloody nose. That was the last time that he ever bullied me. I had to face my fears and stand up to the bully. The paddling I received from the principal was extremely painful, but totally worth it. And my dad was so proud of me for standing up and fighting back.

In many ways, death is like that bully, standing in our faces threatening to destroy us. Our fear of death can dominate our lives, causing us to go to extreme measures to try to escape from its grasp. But no matter how strong we think we are, or how advanced our medical technology is, death will still show up for us in the end.

I was reminded of this truth in a recent missions trip to Africa. I had been to the Congo and gotten some type of intestinal virus, about which I will spare you the details except to say that afterwards I was nine pounds lighter.[2] The good news was that I lived, but the bad news was that the trip was only halfway over. I was traveling with Caleb, one of my associate pastors, and we were detained in the Johannesburg airport for several hours because we were missing some paperwork we needed to enter South Africa. After three hours, we finally made it through customs, and were greeted by Alan and Carol,[3] our gracious hosts for this part of the trip.

We arrived at their home well past midnight after a full day of travel, and I was still feeling extremely weak from being sick,

---

2. I will forever be grateful for my Pastor friend Dennis who laid hands on me and prayed for me as I lay groaning in my hotel bed with only tighty-whities on. Shortly after his prayer, I experienced a deliverance. Thanks Dennis. You're now in the club.

3. Alan and Carol are Vineyard pastors in Johannesburg, South Africa.

so all I wanted to do was crash. But, trying to be nice, we stayed up talking for a while, getting to know their family. Then, out of nowhere, their daughter shared a story about a recent tragedy.

They had a family cat[4] that lived with them for many years, and it had musical abilities. It would walk on the piano and make what they thought of as some type of wonderful music. The cat was very old and became sickly, so they made the hard decision to put it down. After everyone said their goodbyes, the father and son took the cat to the vet. One night, about two weeks later, they were awakened by the sound of the piano being played just like the cat used to. By this time they had already found another cat to replace the one that they had put down, and they thought, "Wow, how great that our new cat does what the old one did."

Alan, awakened by the music, got up out of bed, walked into the living room, and flipped on the lights, only to discover that it was the old cat back from the dead! Upon seeing Alan, the cat glared at him and let out a low, almost guttural, Stephen King type meow. With goose bumps springing up all over, he was shocked to see the needle still stuck in the cat's leg, connected to a frayed IV that the cat had obviously chewed through but which was still taped securely to its fur.

Somehow, after escaping from the gas chamber at the vet, this cat (we could call him Rocky) crawled all the way home, over fifteen miles away. We were shocked by this incredible story and asked Pastor Alan what they did with the cat that came back from the dead. In a matter-of-fact way, Alan responded that the next day he and his son took the cat back to the vet, and this time they stayed to witness the execution. Talk about no mercy; even in all my dislike of cats I thought that after all he did to survive, the cat deserved to live at least a little longer. But in the end, death had

---

4. She lost me at the mention of the word *cat*, as I have no love for cats.

its way. We slept very little that night, listening for the sound of piano music.

As a pastor for over thirty years now, I know that there is a real pain and sorrow that accompanies death. Whether it is a nineteen-year-old killed in a motorcycle accident; a twenty-year-old lost to suicide; a fifty-five-year-old church elder to brain cancer; Geoff, one of my best friends, to ALS; or maybe just old age that has taken one of your loved ones — death touches all of us. I have presided over far too many funerals, filled with unimaginable grief. Just recently, I preached two memorials in two weeks for two of the best and most loved people we have ever had in our church.[5] It is in these moments that all of us must choose to face the bully. The grief for both families is overwhelming, yet they don't let fear shove them around. They have a hope in Jesus as the one who stood up to this bully called death and defeated it.

When Jesus died on the cross, he allowed death to take its best shot at him. It's just like that classic scene in the first *Star Wars* movie (the real first one). Obi Wan, who was Luke Skywalker's mentor, was fighting the evil Darth Vader when he shockingly dropped his light saber — leaving himself completely vulnerable for Darth to strike the fatal blow. At the last moment, Obi Wan warns Darth that, "If you strike me down, I will become more powerful than you can possibly imagine." Vader fails to believe the warning, and, to his own future destruction, strikes the fatal blow. In the same way, Jesus dropped his light saber, his infinite power as Creator and Lord of the universe, and laid down his life, allowing death to strike its fatal blow. Yet, three days later, Jesus

---

5. Chuck served on my church council and was one of the most respected leaders in our church, as well as being one of our worship leaders. He was known as the "sax man" because he could play a mean saxophone. Polly was a single mom in our church and an educator in our community who was deeply respected by all of her fellow teachers.

came out of the grave, ultimately defeating the power of death. An old Puritan preacher described Jesus' victory as "The Death of Death in The Death of Christ."[6] The writer of Hebrews described Jesus' victory this way: "... So that by his death he might destroy him who holds the power of death — that is, the devil — and free those who all their lives were held in slavery by their fear of death" (Heb 2:14-15).

Faith in Jesus does not exempt us from death, but gives us the promise of overcoming it. At the cross, Jesus took the "sting" out of death (1 Cor 15:56). Death still buzzes around us, trying to intimidate, but it has no stinger. "Even though I walk through the valley of the shadow of death, I will fear no evil, *for* you are with me" (Ps 23:4, emphasis added).

I could depress you with far too many tear-filled stories, but I'm sure you already have too many of your own. I don't want to take you on a depressing journey about death, but I want to celebrate the hope we have in Jesus. Together, let's give Ugly Death a punch in the nose by finding ways to laugh in its face.

*   *   *

I want to welcome you into the ugly world of death from a pastor's warped perspective.[7] Sometimes we experience healing just by laughing.[8] It tells the bullies in our lives that they do not intimidate us. So lighten up — you may feel guilty about laughing at such a serious subject, but give it a try. You might find that it is

---

6. John. Owen, *The Death of Death in The Death of Christ* (Edinburgh: The Banner of Truth Trust, 1967).

7. I must confess to having inappropriate humor, so please try to forgive me.

8. Reinhold Niebuhr once said, "Humor is in fact the prelude to faith, and laughter is the beginning of prayer."

like medicine. "A cheerful spirit is good medicine" (Prov 17:22).[9]

As a new pastor, fresh out of seminary, I had studied the ethics of cremation, but no one had trained me on how to spread ashes. Performing the actual service for someone who was cremated was not much different than a funeral with a casket, except you had this small pot, called an urn, instead of the traditional coffin. What no one prepared me for was all the ways people choose to spread the ashes of their loved ones.

My first attempt at spreading the ashes happened to be on a boat. The dearly departed loved the water and wanted to have his ashes scattered out in the deep. Well, my first problem was that I get seasick very easily, and I was starting to feel woozy soon after leaving the dock. It didn't help that on the way out some of the grandkids opened up the urn and began to examine and play with the ashes. One of them held up a large piece of Grandpa and proclaimed, "This looks like one of Grandpa's toes!"[10] At this point I was beginning to wonder, "What I have gotten myself into?"

Shortly after that, we arrived at the spot for the sea burial, and then all eyes were on me, the "expert."[11] I began acting like I knew what I was doing — I read some verses out of the Bible and made a few comments. Now I had to figure out what came next. I decided that when all else failed, just act religious. So I dug in and took a large handful of Grandpa[12] out of the urn so that I could scatter

---

9. I have read through the Bible a few times, and believe it or not, laughter is not a sin!

10. I was actually surprised to see such large pieces in the ashes. And, of course, this bone picking did nothing to ease my seasickness.

11. They had no idea it was my first time!

12. Just a little trivia knowledge for you: cremation ashes are rarely all from just one person. It costs too much to cremate one body at a time, so they cremate several at a time. This creates quite the mixture!

his ashes. It never entered my mind to pay attention to which direction the wind was blowing before I proclaimed with great authority, "In the name of the Father, the Son, and Holy Spirit, we release Grandpa back to You, Lord." I then threw Grandpa's ashes into the wind, but before I could close my mouth, Grandpa came flying back into my face! I had Grandpa in my mouth, eyes, and up my nose. I began to gag, and nearly threw up as the family screamed in horror. I was so embarrassed! What a rookie move. At least, in all of the excitement, I got over my seasickness.[13]

If we listen to the bully, then the ashes can seem to scream out in their silence, "Death has won and life is meaningless." I often hear grieving people mutter things like, "What a waste" or "his life was too short" or "Why, of all times, now?" Only Jesus can turn the silent screams of Ugly Death into songs of beauty.

* * *

After years of all kinds of memorials, and disposing of people's ashes in every imaginable location, I thought nothing else could shock me, but I was wrong. A man I had reached out to with the good news of Jesus many years earlier had died. I had no contact with him for twenty years and could barely remember him. Apparently, he had not forgotten me though, and in his will he had requested that I spread his ashes by the lighthouse on the beautiful resort island of Sanibel, Florida,

---

13. Later it struck me (in my sick mind) that I may have stumbled on a cure for seasickness — snorting Grandpa! I thought of a marketing name for my new discovery: *Ole Granddad.* "Just a pinch between the cheek and gum, and no more sea sickness for you!" Even now as I write this years later, I can still taste Grandpa in my mouth; we are forever bonded. It makes me think of that hauntingly sad song from the rock group Kansas: "Dust in the wind, all we are, is just dust in the wind." I also read that Keith Richards, in a drug stupor, once snorted some of his grandfather's ashes. At least Keith could blame it on the drugs.

where I had been a pastor for seventeen years.[14]

I met the family at the selected spot on the island in front of the lighthouse. As we walked to the beach, they told me how much I had meant to their father. All that I could remember about him was that he had a terrible alcohol problem back when I had tried to help him. While they were telling me about his last wishes, they pulled out a brown paper bag, which I assumed contained an urn — but out came a bottle of Jack Daniels filled with his ashes. I was taken completely off guard!

They said that their father had requested that his ashes be placed inside the Jack Daniels bottle with a personal note that he had written, and he wanted me to cast it out to sea. It was like burying a person inside the weapon that had killed them. Why does God let me get into these weird situations? Maybe in my younger years I might have been able to do it, but with the familiar taste of Grandpa's ashes still in my mouth, I had to say no to throwing the Jack Daniel's bottle into the water.

I told them I would pray and read some Scripture, but they would have to throw Dad out to sea. They were hurt, but went ahead and sent Dad out with all their love.

Thank God the tide was going out so that the bottle floated away. I have often wondered who found this bottle and what the message could have said inside. It would be just like the Lord to use something like a bottle of Jack Daniels with someone's ashes inside to change a person's life.

Can you imagine a fisherman, out to sea, overcome by addictions and the loss of his family, alone on a boat with a loaded gun, desperately petitioning God for a sign — something to give him a reason to go on? Then, here comes Ole Jack Daniels with a message from God:

---

14. Fingerprints!

Whoever finds this bottle, this message is for you from a dying man. I once tasted of the grace of God, years ago, and then turned my back on Jesus for many years. I lost my family, friends, and most of all, my faith. As I stare death in the face, I am filled with much fear, but I have cried out to Jesus again and, in his great mercy, He has heard my cries and forgiven me. I am at peace with God, and ready to die, but I wanted my life to make a difference in someone before it is too late. So if you are reading this, you must be that person. Just as Samson killed more enemies of God in his death than he did in life; so I hope to strike a blow for Jesus as I breathe my last breath. Don't waste your life living for you; make an Ugly Exchange with Jesus. Give him your messed-up life in exchange for his eternal life. I have prayed for this message to find you; Sincerely, Jack.

I would not be surprised to meet someone in heaven who found faith in Jesus from a message in a bottle. Maybe even a message in an ugly book will find its way into the hands of one who is lost, needing a Carl to help them find their path out of their Fort Wilderness. Death is ugly, but God is always able to bring beauty out of the worst circumstances. All I can do is laugh and leave all of our craziness in God's hands.

* * *

My favorite Ugly Death story comes from a friend and fellow pastor. This pastor was asked to do a favor for one of his church members by performing a memorial service for a lady who had died in their city.[15] So, being a good pastor, he went to bury this person he had never met. As he knocked on the door, he was thinking, "Please God, help me get this over with quickly so I can get home to my family." To his surprise, a woman resembling Mrs. Doubtfire answered the door.[16] As quickly as she opened the door — her hair

15. These are some of the hardest funerals because you do not know anything about the person that died, and yet the family still expects you to make it personal.

16. If you have not seen Robin William's playing the part of an old

in a large bun that tilted to one side as she leaned to the other — it became obvious that she had been drinking way too much, trying to drown the sorrow of losing her loved one. As the pastor introduced himself, with his most reverent, calm, spiritual sounding voice, "Hello, I am Pastor..." she blurted out in her high-pitched, thick English accent, "It's all ... bullshit! It's all ... bullshit!"

Now, at this point, any spiritual pastor is praying, "How can I minister to this grieving woman who happens to look and sound like Mrs. Doubtfire?" While, in reality, this pastor was thinking, "I want to kill the church member who got me into this." But, as good pastors do, he faked concern and stepped into the *Twilight Zone* of Ugly Death.

Apparently, Mrs. Doubtfire was the daughter of the lady that had died. She was not taking it well, and she continued shouting, "Why did mother have to die? Why did God take mother away from me? It's all ... bullshit!" The pastor attempted in vain to console her, but she was not exactly open to any spiritual counsel. The pastor finally took charge and herded everyone into the backyard for the service. The backyard was on a canal. They had chairs set up facing a lectern, and in front of the lectern were balloons tied to some kind of a big bowl. As the pastor got closer, he realized that it was a silver gravy dish containing mother's ashes and it was engraved with the words *Bon Voyage*.[17]

At the sight of the balloons, Mrs. Doubtfire went off again saying, "It's all ... bullshit!" At this point the pastor became overwhelmed and had to walk to the side, desperately trying to fight off inappropriate laughter. However, this looked to the

---

English Lady in the movie *Mrs. Doubtfire*, please go rent the movie and watch it before reading the rest of this story.

17. I guess that a gravy dish is a step up from the Jack Daniels bottle. I just hope that the gravy bowl was not the weapon that killed Mother.

family like an attempt to collect his thoughts before he spoke. Now, with his whole body shaking, the "man of God" cried out to the Lord for strength to keep him from erupting with laughter and thereby ruining this near-perfect memorial. By the grace of God, he managed to pull together his emotions and give a very forgettable sermon.

After the service, everyone gathered together by the canal for the Bon Voyage send-off for mother. Before the pastor could take charge of the spreading of the ashes, Mrs. Doubtfire stepped up and grabbed a handful of mother out of the gravy dish. In her drunken stupor, she looked as though she might fall into the water at any moment, but to the pastor's surprise, she suddenly decided to become religious! With this newfound faith, she very reverently (yet still slurring the words) proclaimed in her high-pitched English accent, "In the na-hme of the Fah-thurh and of the Suh-uhn and of the Hoo...ly Spirit!" With that, she threw her handful of mother's ashes into the water.

Within seconds, the word was out to all the fish in the canal. They were like piranhas in a feeding frenzy, devouring mother's ashes! At the sight of this, Mrs. Doubtfire began screaming, "O my Gawd! They are eating mother! Someone stop them. They are eating mother!" With that the "man of God" snapped and went over the edge; he began screaming in a very English accent, "maybe it really is all bullshit after all!" (Okay, I made up the last part — he was a better pastor than I would have been. I certainly would have said it!)[18]

If there is no resurrection, and the bully death is the winner,

18. Of course, I came up with a wonderful new product in our Recycled Ashes line. I have already told you about *Ole Granddad*, and *Message in a Bottle Ministries*. Now our newest product is called, *Mum Chum* — It drives fish wild!

then the Bible tells us that it is worse than "It's all bullshit." As the Apostle Paul said, life without hope of the resurrection is empty and meaningless, and Christians "... are to be pitied more than all men" (1 Cor 15:12-19). When Jesus rose from the grave on the third day after his crucifixion, he conquered death and changed everything. Now we have a hope that gives us courage to face death without fear. We know that the bully is beaten by the power of the resurrection of Jesus!

This hope is far more than just going to heaven after we die, as one of my favorite authors, N. T. Wright, points out in his wonderful book *Surprised by Hope*. Bishop Wright points out the truth that Jesus' resurrection was the beginning of the New Creation that God has promised — the restoration of all things. His resurrection promised that our bodies will live again in a new heaven and new earth (2 Pet 3:13) — and this gives hope to all of creation! This hope is the guarantee that nothing we do in Jesus' name is ever wasted. After teaching on the truths of the resurrection for fifty-seven verses,[19] Paul sums it all up with the life-changing promise that the resurrection gives us: "Therefore, my dear brothers and sisters, stand firm. Let nothing move you. Always give yourselves fully to the work of the Lord, because you know that your labor in the Lord is not in vain" (1 Cor 15:58 TNIV). And Bishop Wright illuminates this text, writing:

> Every act of love, gratitude, and kindness; every work of art or music inspired by the love of God and delight in the beauty of his creation; every minute spent teaching a severely handicapped child to read or to walk; every act of care and nurture, of comfort and support, for one's fellow human beings and for that matter one's fellow nonhuman creatures; and of course every prayer, all spirit-led teaching, every deed that spreads the gospel, builds up the church, embraces and embodies holiness rather than corruption, and makes the

---

19. First Corinthians 15 is the longest chapter the Apostle Paul ever wrote.

name of Jesus honored in the world — all of this will find its way, through the resurrecting power of God, into the new creation that God will one day make…. God's recreation of his wonderful world, which began with the resurrection of Jesus and continues mysteriously as God's people live in the risen Christ and in the power of his Spirit, means that what we do in Christ and by the Spirit in the present is not wasted. It will last all the way into God's new world."[20]

Without the promise of resurrection, it's all bullshit. If it offends you to use such harsh, earthy language to describe the hopelessness of life without the hope of resurrection, all I can say is that what ought to make you truly angry are the lies that Ugly Death keeps telling grieving hearts. I hope that you will gladly step both of your feet right in middle of the pile of the B.S. that Satan is speaking as he tells everyone that he has won. Punch him in the face with the promise of Jesus' resurrection and watch him run away screaming like a little girl. Yes, you may get some nasties on your feet, but it is so worth it when you see hope fill a grieving heart.

In John 11, Jesus walked right into a nasty pile of death's B.S. He stood among grieving family members who had just lost their brother and confronted the lies. As death tried to bully these brokenhearted people, Jesus spoke the truth of who he was — "… I am the resurrection and the life. He who believes in me will live, even though he dies; and whoever lives and believes in me will never die. Do you believe this?" (John 11:25-26). If you have not stepped in a nasty pile of death's lies yet, you will. When you stand, staring at the ashes of a loved one, and they scream out in silence that death has won and it is all in vain, invite the Lord, who is the resurrection, to bring his hope.

"Where, O death, is your victory?

Where, O death, is your sting?" (1 Cor 15:55).

---

20. N. T. Wright, *Surprised by Hope: Rethinking Heaven, the Resurrection, and the Mission of the Church* (New York, NY: Harper One, 2008), 208.

I am ready to accept whatever He gives, and to give whatever He takes with a big smile.
— Mother Teresa

Chapter 7. Ugly Worship

Singing in the Rain

Remember my hitchhiking experience from Ugly Prayer? The time I was picked up by the guy in the Magic Mushroom Mobile? The reason I was going to Fort Myers was to preach at a little Baptist church on Sanibel Island. You never know when small acts of obedience will open greater doors. After the marathon experience of my car breaking down and hitchhiking all the way home, I arrived to preach the next day at this church as their guest speaker. I felt pretty important about being asked to speak to adults because, up to this point, all of my preaching had been to students. There were five cars in the parking lot when I arrived. I thought that the word must not have gotten out about the dynamic young guest speaker that was preaching that day! I don't remember what I spoke about; I only remember the whipping from the Lord I received for complaining about the size of the crowd. He let me know that if I could not be faithful with a few, he would never trust me with more.

Months later, this church decided they wanted a pastor and someone remembered me.[1] By now I had met the love of my life, gotten married, and was finishing seminary. After a little prayer,

---

1. The vote for me to become their pastor was eleven to one. My first message at the church was out of John 6:70, which states, "Have I not chosen you, the Twelve? Yet one of you is a devil!" (Just kidding!)

I announced to my new bride that we were moving (away from all her family) to pastor a church in Sanibel. Kim was a trooper and we loaded up what little we had and moved. It was a spiritual suicide mission to allow this twenty-two-year-old to lead a church with no previous experience, and no mentoring. I had a gift to preach and was filled with passion, but lacked wisdom and was completely unprepared for what lay ahead.[2]

But what I lacked in experience I somewhat made up for with sincere love for Jesus. I had made the Ugly Exchange, and he had rescued me from death and given me new life. I was sold out to him! Early on in my walk with Jesus, I discovered what A. W. Tozer calls the "missing jewel of the evangelical Church"[3] — worship.

* * *

My first experience of connection with the presence of God in worship was a conference called "Jesus '75." This was a gathering of over 15,000 "Jesus Freaks" in a cow pasture just outside Orlando. We gathered in the open air under huge tents to learn about Jesus and to worship him together. If you have never tasted the sweetness of his presence through singing simple love songs to him, I feel sorry for you. This was worship like the prophet Isaiah encountered

---

2. This is why we are so passionate about investing in young leaders today. Mentoring and fathering them is a huge priority to us. Only the spiritually fatherless understand the great need for being fathered. All of my failures (and I had many) were on my own and were very public. It was like learning to walk the tightrope with no safety net. Everything I learned was by trial and error as I experimented on these poor "sheep." I was like the doctor in Frankenstein trying to sew parts of people together to make a church. I longed to hear the words, "it's alive!"

3. A. W. Worship: The Missing Jewel of the Evangelical Church. Christian Publications. Tozer, *Worship: The Missing Jewel of the Evangelical Church.* (Camp. Hill, PA: Christian Publications, n.d.).

in the presence of God, which left him feeling "ruined" (Isa 6:5).[4] Just one taste of the beauty of Jesus in worship will "ruin" you. You will be undone, humbled, and broken; and realizing your sinfulness, you'll be able to sing along with the great hymn, "amazing grace, how sweet the sound."

Worship shows us that we are human: flawed and ugly — because the clearer we see him in worship, the more we realize how unlike him we are. Yet the miracle is that he welcomes us as *Ugly Worshippers* and delights in our praises. The one the birds sing to, the one all creation was made to bring pleasure to, he is the one we worship. The reason we have breath is to worship God. "Let everything that has *breath* praise the Lord" (Ps 150:6, emphasis added). As you draw your next breath and exhale, let praise come forth for the one who sits on the throne.

I brought this passion for authentic, heartfelt worship into a Baptist church that was used to singing hymns with an organ. That quickly changed! I fought more of my battles over worship styles than anything else. People nearly came to blows with me for taking away their hymn books and replacing them with the "evil" overhead projector. You would have thought that I brought an idol into the church![5]

Yet, over time, as a church we began to discover this "jewel" called worship. On one particular Sunday night, we had an Isaiah-like experience together. There were few people there, maybe thirty hungry worshippers; but there was a strong sense of God's presence. At one point in the night, we got stuck on one chorus, caught up in the wonder of his presence, and we sang over and over, "our God

---

4. Another version translates this as "being undone" (KJV), which is also a good translation.

5. Of course, I did everything suddenly and with little warning (and certainly no wisdom) — believe me, I paid for it!

reigns, our God reigns, our God reigns."[6] We concluded with hugs and then headed back to our homes. We went to bed that night filled with joy and peace, still humming "our God reigns" as we drifted off to sleep.

The peace was shattered with a 3 a.m. phone call. Late night calls are never good news. The broken voice said, "Jamie, come quickly. Mark is not breathing!" Then they hung up.

One of my leaders who had been present that night with us in worship had left his wife at home to care for their firstborn son, Mark, who seemed to have a cold. Mark was four years old and best friends with our oldest daughter, Kelly, who was also four. A few weeks earlier, Mark had prayed in Sunday school to give his heart to Jesus. Soon after asking Jesus into his heart, Mark asked his parents if he could be baptized.[7] At this point in my ministry, I had never baptized anyone younger than nine. After giving it some thought (with no handbook on how to handle these things, and no mentor to ask), I said that I felt that Mark was too young and that we should wait before baptizing him. His parents went along with what I said, because I was their pastor, who spoke for God.

Driving to Mark's house, I had only a few minutes to pray and to try to get myself together, but nothing I had ever experienced could have prepared me for what was waiting for me there. As I pulled into the driveway, there were police cars and ambulances everywhere. When I walked into the house, I saw Mark's mother, surrounded by EMS workers, sitting in a chair and holding Mark's lifeless body. She looked up at me with total desperation and collapsed, throwing Mark into my arms screaming, "Jamie! Pray for him! Bring him

---

6. L. E. Jr. Smith, "Our God Reigns," New Jerusalem Music. 1974, 1978. Used by Permission.

7. We believed then, as I still do today, that after someone has surrendered their life to Jesus, making the Ugly Exchange, that they needed to follow Jesus in believer's baptism.

back to life!" I have probably never felt more powerless than I did at that moment. I had never even been around death, let alone touched a dead body.

I had taught on the power of Jesus to work miracles, and now I needed one. It's easy to teach these stories as abstract truths, principles that remain trapped in the Bible. But I had called the church to believe in the impossible, and these people obviously did. But did I?[8]

I held Mark's lifeless body, and with all the faith I could muster, I cried out to Jesus to bring Mark back to life. I rebuked the presence of death, and I called on the power of Jesus who raises the dead. Jesus' words were the reason that I believed in miracles. He had told his followers, "... Anyone who has faith in me will do what I have been doing. He will do even greater things than these, because I am going to the Father" (John 14:12). So I prayed, with two distraught parents looking on in shock, as well as all of the medical personnel. I tried every faith formula that I had ever heard others use; but he was gone! Death was standing over us, screaming, "I won; your faith makes no difference," and at that moment I believed those lies.

Mercifully, one of the EMS workers took Mark's body from me. I don't remember anything that happened after that. The next thing I do remember is driving home on Casa Ybel Road in the pouring rain at around four a.m. I was banging my fist on the dashboard, screaming at God, "Why? Why Mark? He is so young! He loved you! His parents serve you! Why? Why didn't you answer my faith prayers?" Questions and doubts flooded my heart like the rain pouring on the windshield.[9]

---

8. It would be easier if I didn't believe that Jesus still heals and works miracles today — there would be no expectation.

9. I was overwhelmed with personal guilt for not having baptized Mark. Not that that kept him from heaven, but I had robbed his family from experiencing something wonderful together.

The next thing that happened was a defining moment in my spiritual life and has shaped me as a pastor as much as anything I have ever experienced. In my anger and despair, God spoke to me as clearly as I have ever heard him.[10] He didn't offer me any insight into the mystery of his ways, and he had no answers for the cries of my demanding heart. He did not even try to comfort me with gentle words. Instead, he gave me a simple command, "Jamie, sing!" This bizarre message was totally contradictory to all of the doubt, self-pity, and anger I was feeling. Not only did I hear him command me to sing, but he also had a song request.

He told me to sing *Our God Reigns*,[11] and I knew that he meant the same chorus that we had been singing only hours earlier, in the safety of the walls of our church. But at church, we were led by musicians and gifted singers (of which I am neither). To this day, I can't believe it, but I told the Lord "no." It is a major contradiction to tell the Lord of all, "No" since "Yes, Lord," is what a true disciple says to Jesus.

With tears running down my face I said, "No way am I going to sing." I was angry and disillusioned. I know it's arrogant to look into God's face and say no; it is the defiance of unbelief, and the false illusion that God owes us an answer. It is what Eugene Peterson calls Christian idolatry — "using God instead of worshipping God."[12] This is what happens when we reduce God to serving us, fulfilling our desires and answering our prayers. You may feel sorry for me, and you may think that God was being harsh and unloving; but that is the wrong way to see it — because he does comfort us as

---

10. I don't know if what I heard was audible, or if it was that "still small voice," (which can get awful loud).

11. L. E. Jr. Smith, "Our God Reigns."

12. Eugene Peterson, *Living the Resurrection* (Colorado Springs, CO: Navpress, 2006), 33.

no other, and his love heals all of our wounds. This experience was like what one author calls "severe mercy."[13] God was showing me how I only wanted to worship him when it made me feel good or when he served my purposes — and that was painful.

It was a showdown between the God who rules the universe and the pastor — the same guy who once blindly challenged God to prove himself by striking a tree with a lightning bolt. Would I challenge him again to prove himself to me? Would I tell him to make life make sense, to answer all my questions, to be my servant, like Aladdin's genie?[14] Would I be able to control the Lord of all through my faith formulas?

In his mercy, the Father firmly spoke to me a second time: "Sing *Our God Reigns*,"[15] and if you don't do it now, don't ever sing it again." I knew intuitively that God was not just requesting a song because he liked it. He was calling me to worship him. This was so much deeper than a song; he wanted a sacrifice; a complete surrender. True worship always involves some form of a sacrifice. Sometimes this sacrifice is as simple as worshipping when you are not in the mood. Other times, worship calls for us to make great sacrifices — as when God asked Abraham to sacrifice his only son whom he loved more than anything (Gen 22). God asks hard things, and true worshippers, as Mother Teresa said, "refuse him nothing."

Up to this point, I thought that worship was about my experience, what I got out of it. I knew we worshipped because God is great, but I had so easily made worship about Jamie: *Do*

---

13. Sheldon Vanauken, *A Severe Mercy* (New York, NY: Harper and Row, 1977).

14. Except, in this analogy, I rub the Bible and God pops out and asks what I wish for him to do for me.

15. L. E. Smith, Jr., "Our God Reigns."

I like this worship song, or is the electric guitar too loud? Why is it so hot in here? These are examples of pretty worship — which is more about us than it is about Jesus. In pretty worship, we want to sing — to the tune of Matt Redman's worship song, *The Heart of Worship*[16] — "It's all about me! It's all about me, Jamie!" Pretty worship is about the sound, the feelings, the vibe, and the pretty worship leader; and a little about God.

* * *

In the Book of Job, we learn many things, a big one being that God is a terrible negotiator; he refuses to compromise! He never answers a single one of Job's questions. He does just the opposite. He drills Job with question after question. "Do you…? Can you…? Can you...? Can you…? Can anyone…? Where were you…? Do you know...?" (Job 38-41). Finally, Job cries "uncle" and taps out. In the midst of all his loss and suffering, Job's answer to all of God's questions was to lay his understanding at the feet of the one he worshipped.

Trust must replace questions if we are going to move past pretty worship and experience Ugly Worship. Who God is must be enough, or the answers to our questions will become our god. God answered all of the world's suffering — not by giving us explanations — but by entering into our pain and taking our sorrows and sicknesses upon himself. Through Jesus, all of the pain and sin of the world was nailed to the cross. He takes it, and in the Ugly Exchange gives us peace that is beyond all understanding.

I chose, driving in the rain that night on Casa Ybel Road, to worship. I had to pull over to the shoulder, and the tears flowed as I began to sing Ugly Worship out of the sacrifice of obedience:

---

16. Matt Redman, "The Heart of Worship," 1997 Kingsway's ThankYou Music.

Our God reigns, [even though Mark is dead,]
Our God reigns, [even though he did not answer my
    prayers,]
Our God reigns, [even when I do not understand,]
Our God reigns, [even when I do not see him,]
Our God reigns, [even when I do not feel it,]
[Yes,] Our God Reigns.[17]

Peace began to fill my heart — not removing the sorrow or changing the circumstances — but bringing hope. Even through the tears I began to see clearly.

This is faith: not looking with physical eyes, but seeing the unseen. Not believing because I understood, but understanding because I believed. Because, no matter how ugly things are, he is still beautiful. He received my sacrifice of Ugly Worship that night with tears in his eyes, as he smiled over me, confessing to all of heaven, "That is my son, in whom I am well pleased." Over the years, I have been singing in the rain through the disillusionments, sorrows, and ugliness of life. By his grace, I will continue to offer God my sacrifice of Ugly Worship.

* * *

As a young pastor, I had the privilege of being invited to join a group that got to have lunch with an older man of God that I greatly respected. I had so many questions that I wanted to ask him. I wanted to know what he had learned over the many years of walking with Jesus. He threw all of us off when he started sharing about what he wrote in his Bible. He told us that he always placed question marks by the verses and stories that he did not understand (either he didn't understand what they meant, or he could not figure out what God was up to). He said that the longer that he walked with Jesus, the more (not less) questions he

---

17. L. E. Smith, Jr., "Our God Reigns."

had. He told us that his Bible was covered with question marks on every page. We had hoped that with maturity would come certainty in our faith, only to hear the opposite.

After many years of seeking and following Jesus, I have found this to be my experience, too. It does not weaken my faith to have more questions than answers; it strengthens it. I have learned that my faith does not rest on my own understanding (Prov 3:5-6), but it rests in Jesus, in whom I have placed all my trust. When we asked what the old pastor did with all of his questions, he replied, "I do the same thing with them as I do with my sins. I lay them down at the cross at the feet of Jesus and I worship him." That is Ugly Worship!

Let me close this painful chapter with a wonderful story called "Signing in the Cesspool" that Sam Storms records in his book *The Singing God*:[18]

> At a conference in Brighton, England, in 1991, a remarkable word of testimony was given by a pastor from China. He had spent eighteen years in a prison for his faith. Here is a man who seemed to have every reason to doubt God's love for him, but he didn't.
>
> "His assigned task in the camp was to empty the human waste cesspool …. Listen as this remarkable man of God describes his experience:
>
> 'It was more than two metres in breadth and two metres in length, filled with human waste collected from the entire camp. Once it was full, the human waste was kept until it was ripe and then dug out and sent to the fields as fertilizer. Because the pit was so deep I could not reach the bottom to empty it; I had to walk into the disease-ridden mass and scoop out successive layers of human waste, all the time breathing the strong stench. The guards and all the prisoners kept a long way off because of the stench.
>
> 'So why did I enjoy working in the cesspool? I enjoyed the solitude. In the labour camp all the prisoners normally were

18. Sam Storms, *The Singing God* (Orlando, FL: Creation House, 1998), 94.

under strict surveillance and no one could be alone. But when I worked in the cesspool I could be alone and could pray to our Lord as loudly as I needed. I could recite the Scriptures.... Also I could sing loudly the hymns I still remembered.

'In those days one of my favourites was 'In the Garden.'... When I worked in the cesspool I knew and discovered a wonderful fellowship with our Lord. Again and again I sang this hymn and felt our Lord's presence with me....

'He never left me nor forsook me. And so I survived and the cesspool became my private garden.'"

"In The Garden" by Austin Miles[19]

> I come to the garden alone,
> While the dew is still on the roses;
> And the voice I hear, falling on my ear,
> The Son of God discloses.
> And He walks with me, and He talks with me,
> And He tells me I am His own;
> And the joy we share as we tarry there
> None other has ever known.

This is the experience of Ugly Worship! The next time you find yourself neck-deep in the crap of life, try it. You will discover the Beauty of God, even in the midst of a cesspool. Worshipping in the rain does not stop the rain from falling, it lifts our eyes to the one who Reigns over all. Yes, our God reigns!

---

19. Words and Music by Austin Miles, *In The Garden* (Public Domain).

....

Draw Christ as deep as possible into the flesh.
— Martin Luther

Chapter 8. Ugly Jesus

A Slob Like Us

Jamie, you've gone too far with this ugly thing; it is near-blasphemy to call Jesus ugly! I know this is what you're thinking, because it was screaming in my mind as I wrote this chapter. But first of all, if it does offend God, he can take care of himself. The God of the Bible doesn't need anybody to defend him. Our God is patient, long-suffering, and can take a joke!

There are people who mock everything sacred about the cross of Jesus in the name of entertainment: artists who place a crucifix upside down, "baptizing" it in a large glass container filled with urine — calling it art; comedians on the Academy Awards telling Jesus to f*** off. Now, if I were God, I would squash them like bugs, smearing their guts all around to make a point.[1] I'm sure at this point you are very grateful that I am not God!

I rampaged through all my theology books desperately hoping to find someone who saw this crazy insight of Jesus being ugly, but they all just danced around it. After describing this chapter to a friend of mine who is a pastor, he said he thought Donald Miller had said something about Jesus being ugly in his book, *Searching for God Knows What*. Miller comments on a Scripture

---

1. This reminds me of a cartoon that I saw, where a hippy was holding a sign that said, "God is dead." The next picture showed a giant thumb coming from heaven, squashing him like a bug.

from Isaiah 53: "It seems odd to me that God would want us to know Jesus was unsightly. It was as though the way Christ looked was part of the message he was to communicate."[2] To my relief, there was another person who shared some of my crazy ideas. This does not necessarily make me right, but I feel a little safer. It is never good to do stupid stuff alone. If you are going to take off your clothes and go streaking, don't go solo!

Joan Osborne stirred up the religious community (which is regularly in need of a laxative for its spiritual constipation) in the 1990s with a wonderful song.[3] She sings, like an Old Testament prophet, with a haunting question, "How far did God go in becoming one of us? Could God have gone so far that he could be described as a slob?" Many religious leaders choked on the thought of using the word "slob" to describe God. They said it was irreverent, crude, and near-blasphemy — they had a real "movement" over her song. (Why is it that the first thing religious people lose is their sense of humor? They are too blocked up — like the great theologian Doc Holliday says about his enemy after killing him in a gun fight in the movie *Tombstone*, "he was just too high strung.") What this song was suggesting was just too ugly of a concept for them — they couldn't make it fit with their vision of a white, blue-eyed, tall, handsome, *GQ* Jesus. I don't know Joan's beliefs or background, but I think she presents us with a soul-searching question: Can we dare believe Jesus was really just like us "... in every way?" (Heb 2:17).

Most people get their understanding of what is theologically called *the incarnation of Christ* from pretty Christmas cards. The incarnation, the event of God becoming human, was a messy

---

2. Donald Miller, *Searching for God Knows What* (Nashville, TN: Nelson Books, 2004), 125.

3. Joan Osborne, *One of Us*, Relish (Mercury, 1995).

miracle. In the mystery of the incarnation, Jesus chose to lay aside his rights and privileges as God. He stripped himself of all of his kingly garments of glory and put on the humble garment of flesh, the clothes of a servant, and became poor for us (Phil 2:6-8, and 2 Cor 8:9). Jesus came to earth in the disguise of a "slob," just a normal dude — one of us. The Old Testament prophet Isaiah tried to warn us that the coming Messiah would not look like what we would expect a Messiah to look like: "... He had no beauty or majesty to attract us to him, nothing in his appearance that we should desire him" (Isa 53:2).

There was "*nothing*," about Jesus physically that made him stand out. The appearance of Jesus did not make people think, "Wow, that guy is so spiritual. I would like to hang out with him." Or "I would love to hook up with him; he looks just like Brad Pitt." The prophet Isaiah was, in a nice way, saying, Jesus was not going to look like a normal Jewish man. He would fall far below normal on the beauty scale. And as far as the power and image meter goes, he's not even going to register.

Jesus was not taller, stronger, faster, or better looking than anyone. My guess is that in Mrs. Yentil's fifth grade class at Nazareth Elementary, when they were picking teams for "Hebrew Dodge Ball," Jesus, like Randy, was chosen last. He may have even heard some of the painful words of rejection that Randy endured — "Ha, Ha, you got stuck with Jesus on your team. What a loser!" Years later, those people probably felt like the high school basketball coach who showed his eye for talent by cutting Michael Jordan from the team.

Throughout Christian history, there have been all kinds of attempts to portray Jesus as, tall, sexy, blue-eyed, and, of course, white — kind of like a spiritual Fabio. Is this how the girls in high school viewed Jesus? I imagine that the girls growing up with Jesus were not quite sure what to do with him. They felt safe around him; never feeling a stare of lust,[4] or any attempt to use them, and he never made fun of them for being just "girls." His kind, gentle, honest way was certainly attractive; but they could not see past his ugliness. Who wants to go to a dance with a short, homely guy that comes from a poor family?

I believe that Jesus experienced the same harsh rejection that kids experience from their ruthless peers today, mocking the discovery of any flaws or weaknesses. He may have suffered with jokes about having a big nose that "looks like a camel's nose," or ears that "look like a donkey's ears." Jesus may have suffered from pimples just like most adolescent kids. Even in his early years, Jesus was learning the pain of growing up in a world that worshiped superficial beauty, strength, and wealth. He was experiencing the cost of choosing to be identified with the outcasts of society; of being called a slob just like they were.

I really feel that this is what Isaiah was trying to give us insight into. As a teenager, Isaiah received his call to be a prophet with a dramatic experience of seeing Jesus in all his pre-incarnate glory (Isa 6). The Gospel of John, hundreds of years later, made clear that what Isaiah experienced was the glory of Jesus when John wrote, "Isaiah said this because he saw Jesus' glory and spoke about him" (John 12:41). The result of Isaiah's experience with the glory of Jesus was to be left, in his own words, "ruined."

Isaiah saw himself in the light of the glory of who Jesus was — and Isaiah hit a sprinkler and fell down hard, finding himself lying naked before a Holy God. All Isaiah could say, as he marveled at

---

4. This is not to imply that Jesus was never sexually aroused. As Hebrews 4:15 says, Jesus was "tempted in every way, just as we are — yet was without sin." In fact, he was tempted far beyond what we have ever experienced. Because he never yielded to temptations, Jesus felt the full force of the pull of the temptations.

this glorious Jesus, was, "Woe is me!" (Isa 6:5, KJV). He was being broken. Like grapes, the sweetness doesn't come until after the crushing. What feels like being brutally broken often transforms us into people who are more like Jesus.

Later on in his ministry, Isaiah had a different vision of Jesus. This time he saw into the future and described Jesus as a human that would come to earth to be our Messiah. He saw a suffering servant, "... a man of sorrows, ..." someone who would heal us "...by his wounds ..." (Isa 53:3-5). Before Isaiah penned his wonderful prophetic promise of Jesus coming to suffer for us so we could be saved from our sins, he described Jesus with these words: "He grew up before him … like a root out of dry ground ..." (Isa 53:2). Let me just say that that is a long way from how Isaiah saw Jesus in Chapter 6 — on a throne in all his glory. Now he sees Jesus as a "root out of dry ground!" Have you ever seen a pretty root? At least he could have seen him as a flower or a fruit tree, but instead he saw a gnarly desert root. Roots are not pretty; they are best hidden underground, in the dirt, doing their job to support a beautiful tree. In the Bible, roots most often speak of one's origins, lineage, or family tree, and that is what Isaiah was speaking of here — Jesus had ugly roots.

When I was in seminary, a few of us white boys snuck out to hear a black pastor named E. V. Hill. What a prince of preachers he was; no white man could preach like him. He spoke on "roots," except he pronounced the word "ruts." Pastor Hill used the Alex Haley miniseries *Roots* as the background for his message. The series traced an African family as they were taken out of Africa as slaves. The family was then held in the bondage of slavery for many generations here in America.

Pastor Hill said that the problem with the film was that it did not go back far enough! He proceeded to trace history backwards through the Bible, character by character, until he arrived at the beginning in the Garden of Eden with Adam. He helped us see that "we all come from the same *rut* and it is a rotten *rut!*" He climaxed his message with the call for us to "receive a *rut* transplant." He used quotes from both Isaiah and the Apostle Paul who both spoke of Jesus as the "... Root of Jesse," (Isa 11:10, and Rom 15:12).

Jesse was King David's father, and God had made a promise to King David that his "seed" or lineage, would sit on the throne forever (2 Sam 7:11-16). This "seed" is the Messiah, Jesus — the root out of dry ground. Pastor Hill's call was for all of us to exchange roots with Jesus. He was asking us to give up our rotten roots inherited from Adam, and then be "grafted" (Rom 11:17) onto the true Vine, which is just another way of describing what it means to be born again.

As the Prophet Isaiah traced the lineage of the Messiah back to the "root" of King David, both the Gospels of Matthew and Luke traced back the "roots" of Jesus (Matt 1:1-17, and Luke 3:23-38). The Gospel of Luke, like Pastor Hill's sermon, follows the "roots" of Jesus all the way back to the rotten root of the first man, Adam. The gospel lineages of Jesus are filled with people that you would not want to boast of having in your bloodline. There are adulteresses, hookers, liars, and even murderers. Jesus had ugly roots!

It reminds me of a wonderful scene from *Hitch*. In the movie, Will Smith plays a cool character called "The Date Doctor." He is an expert in women, and especially how to get a date with one that seems way out of reach. In one scene, Smith is attempting to get all of his expertise to work for himself so he can impress this beautiful, hard-to-get girl by planning a "perfect" first date. After researching everything about her, he decides on a plan that he's certain will impress.

He takes her by Jet Ski to Ellis Island, which is where all of the first immigrants from Europe landed. He had researched her ancestry and discovered that one of her relatives who immigrated to America had arrived at Ellis Island and signed the book of remembrance. This book is kept at the museum on the island. So he pulled some strings to get the guard to open the museum on Sunday, just for the two of them. He surprises her by having the book opened to the page with the signature of her first relative that arrived in America. In the book, the signature was followed with the words; "the Butcher of Cadiz." He thought it was just describing the man's occupation, until his date, upon discovering the name of her relative in the book runs out of the building screaming and crying. As it turns out, her relative was a notorious ax murderer! Her family never spoke about him, keeping it hidden as a dark secret that they all wanted to forget. That is a rotten root! As Pastor Hill passionately proclaimed to us, "we all come from rotten *ruts*."

The lineage of Jesus found in the third chapter of Luke's Gospel makes no attempt to airbrush over the uglies of his bloodline.[5] This "dry ground" he sprang up from included a woman who pretended to be a prostitute so that she could seduce her father-in-law and bear his child (the story of Tamar in Genesis 38). There was a hooker who saved her family by hiding Hebrew spies in her brothel in Jericho (the story of Rahab in Joshua 2). There was a woman who was seduced by a King to commit adultery (the story of Bathsheba in 2 Samuel 11). There was the king who committed adultery with Bathsheba and murdered her husband (the story of King David in 2 Samuel 11). Then there was the playboy, King

---

5. The ugliness of the Bible is one of the strongest evidences of divine inspiration as it includes the weaknesses, failures, sinfulness, and complete stupidity of God's best followers.

Solomon (1 Kings 11). Last, but not least, there was a teenage girl who got pregnant out of wedlock and then made up a fantastic story of still being a virgin; claiming that the baby came from the Holy Spirit — Jesus' mother, Mary (Luke 1-2. Just to clarify; I do believe that all of these stories are true).

Along with this ugly bloodline came an ugly birth. Of course, we gloss over these blemishes to make the whole thing look pretty so that Hallmark can sell sentimental Christmas cards. However, in reality, it was a poor, teenage couple that was surrounded with controversy, and rejected from every inn they tried to check into. They finally found a stable (which was occupied by animals), and Mary gave birth while inhaling giant whiffs of nasty animal poop. They then found an old, dirty blanket to wrap the newborn in. In the Christmas cards, Jesus, fresh from the womb, looks ready to model for Baby Gap. The only people who bothered to come check the baby out were the shepherds — who were notoriously dishonest and shady characters. This was an ugly birth for the "Word [made] flesh!" (John 1:14). God wrapped himself in an ugly blanket of flesh and disguised his glory as a Jewish baby. The ways of God are certainly not our ways; they are "foolishness" (1 Cor 2:14) to the wise of this world.

Jesus grew up in an ugly family. He was raised in a poor carpenter's home where he learned the trade of his stepfather, Joseph. There was certainly no boast in those days for being a carpenter. Why didn't God have his Son raised by a doctor, lawyer, business leader, teacher, artist, a politician, or even a king? Jesus lived as a simple, hard-working, single, calloused-handed carpenter for most of his adult life. He spent that time faithfully working to support his mother. He was just a "root out of dry ground." He was so ordinary that no one paid any attention to him; He was just Ugly Jesus.

Not only did Jesus have an ugly bloodline, an ugly birth, an ugly appearance, and an ugly family; but God sent him on an ugly mission too! Jesus " ... did not come to be served, but to serve, and to give his life as a ransom for many" (Mark 10:45). He walked among his creation unrecognized. The creator himself was seen only as a humble servant who identified with the outcasts; washed his disciples' feet; touched the lepers; hung around the "lost sheep" of society; and ate, drank, and laughed with notorious sinners. Jesus never owned a home, never wrote a book, and only had the clothes on his back. He was spit on, he was mocked, and his life ended in the shame of a bloody execution reserved for the worst criminals. That was an ugly mission — an assignment from God that he willingly accepted and joyfully fulfilled.

Why all of this ugliness? Why did God hide the glory of his one and only Son behind the veil of humanity when Jesus was sent to reveal the Father to us (John 1:18)? It was because God loves to hide from the eyes of prideful and unbelieving people. Jesus understood this, and that's why he didn't throw a pity party when people rejected his message. In one instance, he broke out into a dance, shouting, " ... I praise you, Father, Lord of heaven and earth, because you have *hidden* these things from the wise and learned, and *revealed* them to little children. Yes, Father, for this was your good *pleasure*" (Matt 11:25-26, emphasis added). This is The Power of Ugly!

God hid Jesus in the ugly package of a normal human body — just a slob like one of us — so that the true beauty of God could only be seen if the viewers put on new glasses. We must look with new eyes — eyes that have been opened by his Spirit, eyes of faith — if we are going to see through the veil of ugly that hides his glory. Only the humble and childlike will see the beauty of his unconditional love, the glory of his humility, the majesty of his justice, the awesomeness of his power, the wonder of his teaching, and the miracle of his mercy. There is no one like Jesus, who perfectly reflects the beauty of God.

When the woman caught in adultery (John 8),[6] lying naked at the feet of Jesus in all of her guilt and shame, looked up in fear, she looked into the beautiful face of God. She did not see a face that was contorted in angry condemnation, but one with a radiating smile of grace.[7] She saw through the veil of Christ's humanity into the face of God and recognized her Savior. She saw the glory and wonder of God's grace in all its multi-faceted beauty: forgiveness, mercy, kindness, patience, and a love that covered all of her shame and nakedness. The eyes of Jesus became portals into "... the light of the world ...." (Matt 5:14) and she saw a Father who would love her forever. Have you ever seen this smile?

The ultimate ugliness of Jesus' life was witnessed in the Ugly Death that he chose to suffer. Mel Gibson, in *The Passion of the Christ*, may have missed it, casting a handsome, masculine actor to play Jesus, but Gibson got it right in portraying the Ugly Death he suffered. Gibson used the words found in Isaiah to develop the gruesome suffering the film portrays: "Just as there were many who were appalled at him — his appearance was so disfigured beyond that of any man and his form marred beyond human likeness" (Isa 52:14). Most Biblical scholars, as the film *The Passion* does, apply these words to describe the torment and suffering that Jesus endured.[8]

---

6. This story is also referred to in *Ugly Jamie*.

7. Remember though, this condemned woman did not see a handsome, blue-eyed male who would make a great romantic partner — she saw Ugly Jesus.

8. There was a legend in the Middle Ages that proposed that these verses in Isaiah spoke of Jesus having some form of leprosy or deformity. There are no facts to support this claim, and I do not believe this is true. However, maybe you should ask yourself, "would it make any difference in your love for Jesus if,

Just as God hid the glory of Jesus in human weakness, so the kingdom he brought is hidden in ugliness. Who has ever heard of an all-powerful king whose kingdom could be rejected? Who has ever heard of a king who acted like a humble servant and allowed himself to be mocked and spit on? What kind of a king can be put on a cross in total shame and defeat and yet claim to be completely victorious?

Jesus planted the power of his kingdom in the ugly soil of the church. He entrusted the mission of extending his kingdom to a small group of weak disciples. And God continues to hide his power and glory in weak vessels — "... jars of clay" (2 Cor 4:7). This is why his church will always be a weak people, who, like their Lord Jesus, will have "... no beauty or majesty to attract us to him" (Isa 53:2). We must stop trying to be a church that is filled with human strength and beauty that vainly hopes the world will be attracted to it. If the Son of God was unattractive to the world, how can we ever think that we are going to make the church desirable?

Just as a pretty Jesus on a Christmas card will never save anybody, neither will a pretty church. To reach this world will take a flawed church that has experienced God's mercy and is completely dependent upon his Spirit to fill them. In this way, everyone will know that the "... all-surpassing power is from God and *not* from us" (2 Cor 4:7, emphasis added). We will reach a hurting world when we allow him to release his power through the broken cracks of our ugly "jars of clay."

---

while he was on earth, he looked like the Elephant Man? Is our love so shallow that we only love things that are appealing to the eyes of our pride? What if God loved us like that? We would all be without hope, for there is nothing in any of us that attracts God to love us. Spiritually, we all look like the Elephant Man — we all give God plenty of reasons to hate and reject us — but he always responds with love.

As many continue to mock and reject the church in all of its weaknesses, let's join Jesus in his dance of praise and celebration to the Father because he has hidden his glory from the proud and revealed it through The Power of Ugly.

Whoever cannot stand being in community
should beware of being alone.
— Deitrich Boenhoeffer

Chapter 9. Ugly Church

A Whore and My Mother

"Kumbaya, My Lord, Kumbaya; Oh Lord, Kumbaya."

"This little light of mine, I'm going to let it shine…don't let Satan blow it out, I'm going to let it shine, let it shine, let it shine."

"Is this the spiritual version of the *Twilight Zone*?" I wondered as I sat in a stranger's living room. It was my first experience in a Christian youth group, and I was surrounded by the people I made fun of in high school. Didn't anybody know "Stairway to Heaven," "Freebird," or anything with an electric guitar?

When I surrendered my life to become a follower of Jesus, I guess I didn't read the fine print. No one told me that being a Christian meant joining a family made up of weak, broken, and often, weird people. It felt wrong when these people began referring to me as one of the family, or calling me brother. Was I now part of some cult made up of losers?

But God chose me to play on his ugly team. "Of course he picked me," I thought, "He needs my strengths — I mean, *look* at these people!" As I surveyed the living room, sizing up the rest of the group, all of us singing these stupid songs, I had a flashback to Mrs. Hyde's fifth grade class. I was stuck with the rejects again. These people were not the "who's who" of our community — they were not the hippies, jocks, cheerleaders, or generally cool people that I was used to hanging around. It felt like being in a room full of Carls!

For some strange reason, they loved me in spite of how I felt about them. They accepted me around their campfire even though I hadn't brought any good weed. All I really brought to the party was pride, pain, and ugliness. The difference between my new family and my old friends was that they would not leave me lying naked on the ground after hitting a sprinkler. These new friends knew my sins and my reputation, yet they welcomed me anyway. These people knew how to do the "backward walk of love," to help cover my ugliness.

They were like a guy named Ananias in the book of Acts who received the ugly (and scary) assignment to go pray for a man named Saul, who had been putting Christians to death. God told Ananias that Saul was one of his children and that he was to go pray for him. The first words out of Ananias's mouth that the blinded and humbled Saul heard as he placed his loving hands on him were; "Brother Saul,..." (Acts 9:17).[1] How healing these words welcoming Saul to the family of Jesus must have been! Having the courage to welcome someone that had been so evil took God's grace — and that was what this group of young Christians showed me.

Several of the students at this group shared that when we were still in high school they had prayed for me for several years. I never knew that anybody had ever prayed for me! They were a part of a Christian group at school that decided to start praying for the person they thought was least likely to ever become a Christian. They picked Jamie. I began to cry — which

---

1. There are his fingerprints again! Paul had planned to put Ananias in prison, yet God turned the tables on him and used Ananias to set Paul free from his religious prison so that Paul could experience the freedom of the grace of God.

is something that a linebacker never does, but I now wore a new uniform.

I put on Jesus' uniform publicly when I was baptized on December 23, 1975, in a very cold Gulf of Mexico. The pastor proclaimed, "Jamie, because of your faith in the Lord Jesus Christ, I baptize you in the name of the Father, The Son, and The Holy Spirit." When I came up out of the water — feeling cleaner than I had ever felt in my life — I was welcomed into this new family with hugs, kisses, and tears. I had given up my old allegiances, family, and friends in the Ugly Exchange to become part of God's family.

We do not baptize ourselves, it's something done to us by God through the grace-filled hands of someone like Ananias. This man baptized Saul — who went on to write almost half of the New Testament and take the message of Jesus around the known world of that day. Ananias is never mentioned again in the Bible, but his simple act of welcoming a notorious sinner into the family of God will be forever celebrated, and hopefully repeated.

* * *

My father-in-law, Rick, is a godly man who has been like a father to me.[2] Rick likes to tell a story about how, back in the days when he had to travel for work, he loved to mess with hotel receptionists. He would start talking to them about how hard it was to be on the road, away from home, and the beautiful wife he missed so much. He would say, with deep sincerity, "I sure do miss my wife, she is the most beautiful woman in the world," then when he had gained their interest, he would ask, "Would you like to see a picture of her?"

When they said yes, he would pull out of his wallet this picture

---

2. I am not just saying that because I am about to pull his pants down and embarrass him!

he'd found of the "World's Ugliest Woman."[3] The shock on people's faces was priceless! They would quickly look at Rick's face to check out his expression, hoping to see him chuckle and let them know that this was a joke, but Rick had a great poker face. He just loved to watch those receptionists, horrified, struggling to come up with something nice to say about his ugly wife.[4] Then one day, as the Lord will do, he turned the tables on Rick.

Rick had a fresh, unsuspecting victim on the line, and he was about to reel her into his trap. But when he pulled out "Miss Ugly" and showed it to this receptionist, she just stared at the picture, face blank. Slowly, tears began to form and flow down her cheeks. Then she broke down sobbing. Rick asked her what was wrong, and between the sobs, she told him, "I wish I could find someone to love me like that. I'm so ugly, and I'm such a mess, that nobody will ever love me that way!"

Rick was standing there with his pants down and no way out except through the gift of repentance. So he, with tears in his own eyes, told the woman the truth about the picture. He apologized and told her that it was a bad joke — which he now deeply regretted ever using. He went on to share with her that there really was someone who loved her just the way she was, someone that saw her as absolutely beautiful, and his name was Jesus. That day she discovered true love, a love that was not based on false beauty or performance; love that was not earned or deserved, but was freely given to her by her heavenly Father. Rick was able to be an Ananias to her and welcome her to the family of broken

---

3. How ugly was she? She was so ugly that, as a child, her momma had to tie a chicken leg around her neck just to get the dogs to play with her! She wasn't just ugly; she was o-o-o-gly!

4. Rick never let on, and always just left people wondering. In real life, however, Rick's wife, Edna, my mother-in-law, is a beautiful Christian woman.

and flawed people who have exchanged their ugly for his beauty. Of course, as part of Rick's repentance, he tore the picture up and threw it away.

*   *   *

My baptism into the family of God began my long journey of learning to love what Jesus loves — and there is nothing that Jesus loves more than his church, which he calls his, "... bride" (Rev 21:2). Over five hundred years ago, a church leader named John Calvin said, "To those to whom [God] is a Father, the church must also be a Mother."[5] I can identify with that quote. I have lived all of my adult life — the good, the bad, and especially the ugly — in community with God's people. My greatest joys and blessings have come from people who are a part of his church, yet this same family has inflicted some of the most heart-wrenching pain of my life.

As I began to pursue God's calling on me to be a pastor, I made it my mission to build a church that was successful, beautiful, and most of all, cool. When I started pastoring the First Baptist Church of Sanibel Florida in 1979, we had twelve members. As you may recall, I was fresh out of seminary, newly married, and clueless about what I was getting into.

I spent the next seventeen years[6] of my life attempting to create the church I'd been dreaming about. I wanted a place that was just like the book of Acts, but of course, minus all of the ugly parts. I didn't want the divisions, lies, prejudice, corruption, and betrayals. I only wanted the good stuff — the power, healings, growth, love, generous sharing, worship, and beauty. Every time I thought that

---

5. John Calvin, *Institutes of the Christian Religion: Book IV* (Public Domain), 1.1.

6. Fingerprints!

I was making progress and the church was starting to look strong, sinners and ugly people kept finding their way in and messing everything up with all their ugliness. If it weren't for the people, I thought, this could really be a beautiful church!

All the leaders that I looked up to seemed to pastor these great, growing, Spirit-filled, successful churches. I went to all their conferences and sat at their feet to discover their Gnostic secrets of "How to Build a Great Church." Pastors can at times be guilty of lusting for false beauty. We search for a pretty church to work in that will help us climb the ladder to becoming a success. We want to be able to write books and speak at conferences. Eugene Peterson described this in his book on Jonah, *Under the Unpredictable Plant*:

> Parish glamorization is ecclesiastical pornography — taking photographs (skillfully airbrushed) or drawing pictures of congregations that are without spots or wrinkles, the shapes that a few parishes have for a few short years. These provocatively posed pictures are devoid of personal relationships. The pictures excite a lust for domination, for gratification, for uninvolved and impersonal spirituality.[7]

After years of much frustration and disillusionment, trying to produce a pretty and successful church — like those that I had lusted after in the beautiful church centerfolds, I had two life-changing experiences. The first happened while I was attending one of these conferences, but this time there was a different kind of leader teaching — his name was John Wimber. He was the founder of the movement of churches called the Vineyard.[8]

John Wimber was one of the most powerful men of God that I have ever met; yet he refused to act like a superstar, and he often

---

7. Eugene Peterson, *Under the Unpredictable Plant* (Grand Rapids, MI: Eerdmans, 1992), 22.

8. I have been a part of this movement for over twenty years now.

just described himself as "a fat man trying to get to heaven." John refused to wear the religious titles that others wanted to place on him. He was just John, and he was willing to expose his uglies. He was my model of how to preach, and he showed me my first example of The Power of Ugly. John was just one of us; one of the guys — he was no big deal — yet he was filled powerfully with the Spirit. This man became the spiritual father and mentor that I longed to have as a young Pastor.[9] He would often say, "If you want to sign up for God to use you powerfully, then you must be willing to look foolish."[10] John taught me to love the whole church, including the parts that I disagreed with, and even those that were embarrassing for me to be identified with.[11]

John was leading a seminar on how to grow your church — a popular topic for young pastors like myself who wanted to be "successful." As John was teaching, he began to ramble off, telling stories that had nothing to do with the topic he was supposed to be teaching.[12] What happened next, as best as I can remember, a frustrated pastor interrupted him, blurting out, "When are you going to tell me how to grow my church?"

John, as only he could, looked down at the pastor with his fatherly smile and then just went back to his story. A few minutes later, he interrupted again, "I came here to learn how to grow my church, not to listen to these stupid stories." At this point,

---

9. Most of what he taught me was not in one-on-one teaching sessions, but with many others. I listened to him teach and watched him model the message of Jesus in a new way — in an ugly way. That was so freeing to me.

10. He called this being "naturally supernatural," which is just another way of describing The Power of Ugly.

11. Remember that Jesus carries a picture of his bride in his wallet, and he proudly displays it to everyone.

12. This was always the best stuff! See Chapter 12, *Ugly Preaching*, for more detail on this style of teaching.

as John would later share, he was becoming angry about these interruptions. But then the Spirit prompted John that he was going to use this man as an illustration for everyone that was there. So John asked this bold interrupter, "Sir, let me ask you a question. How big do you want to grow your church?" The pastor seemed confused, so John repeated his question adding numbers, "Do you want your church to grow to a five-hundred member church, a thousand member church, a fifteen-hundred member church, maybe a two-thousand member church?"

Hearing the number fifteen hundred must have rung his bell, so he blurted out, "Yes! Fifteen hundred would be great." John paused, listened to the still small voice of God, and then looked lovingly at the pastor and said, "Let me ask you this question. Would you be happy if you had fifteen hundred people in your church who were all *just like you?*" This pastor looked like Evander Holyfield had just punched him in the gut.[13] He began to sob and fell to his knees. In a way, he did get punched, but it was the Holy Spirit, and we all felt the blow.

This pastor wanted fifteen hundred people to make him feel successful and significant and to cover over the ugliness of his own life — his secret addictions, lustful fantasies, inner turmoil, unhappy marriage, and fear of failing. At that time, the church that I pastored was just trying to get over the "one-hundred barrier," and I wanted more, just like this pastor, so that I could feel important, too. In fact, this guy was just like every other pastor in the room; we all wanted bigger churches!

John had humiliated him — he'd pulled his pants down in front of all of his peers. This pastor had struck a sprinkler, gone down hard, and was lying naked before everyone. But then John

---

13. It was like watching a balloon get stuck with a needle, or like the witch in the *Wizard of Oz* crying, "I'm melting, I'm melting."

modeled the backward walk of love, and covered over this leader's shame with prayers and words of mercy and healing.

We all repented together that day for lusting after the false beauty of the world, the lies that say, "bigger is better." Our Ugly Prayers became "O God, O God, O God, help! Forgive us, change us, and make us into the pastors that our churches need us to become. Grow us into healthy leaders who only want your glory." John would often say, "I hear pastors talking about taking their cities for Jesus, when I am having a hard enough time trying to take John for Jesus." I can testify that I have been trying to take Jamie for Jesus for over thirty-five years, and there is so much ground left to cover!

One of my treasured memories with John was driving him to the airport and sharing with him one of my ugliest stories (don't worry, I tell this story in Ugly Altars) and hearing him laugh until he cried saying "Jamie, I will never be able to hear you preach without thinking of that story." John is with Jesus now, and I waited until I was over fifty to write this book, just as he recommended. Thank you, John, for being a father, for teaching me to love the whole church, for teaching me to minister from my weaknesses, and for teaching me to tell ugly stories.

The second life-changing experience that helped to begin my recovery from trying to produce a perfect church happened around the same time. I was feeling like a failure before God because I thought that the church that I led was weak and small. I was trying so hard and doing all that I knew to do and it was not getting any better. The heavenly Father gave me a vision — or really, it was a flashback to when I was thirteen years old. I saw myself pitching on a Little League baseball field. What I saw had actually happened to me, so I was reliving a very painful moment in my childhood.

I was pitching for my team, but I was having a hard time with my control. The other team's coach, smelling blood, told his batters to stop swinging at my pitches so that I would walk them. Sports, just like the Christian life, don't work better because you just try harder. I've seen the best players try so hard and just keep playing worse and worse the harder they try. Simply swinging harder or throwing faster seldom produces the desired results. On this day, the harder I concentrated on trying to throw strikes, the worse I threw.[14]

While I was out there having this terrible time on the mound, my dad — who was in the stands — was hollering at me, "Get your head up boy, and start throwing strikes."[15] The more Dad screamed, trying to help me "try harder," the worse I threw. I even started hitting batters! I struck one kid in the head so hard that they had to take him out of the game. I was fighting back tears, totally humiliated.

At this moment in my vision, the Father in heaven said, "Jamie, you need to forgive your dad for pushing you so hard in life." I did not realize how much pain I was still carrying, even so many years later, from his performance-based parenting. When I forgave him, I felt a huge weight lifted from me. Then the Lord said to me, "Jamie, you think I am like your dad; screaming at you from heaven, 'Grow the church, boy! Grow the church! Be holy, son! Be holy.' The truth is, Jamie: I left heaven to take your place, relieving you from the game. I threw a perfect game in your place. I want you to learn to trust me more instead of trying harder. I will grow my church; you just need to be faithful." These words from God

---

14. This was back before people were smart enough to figure out the relief pitcher system, so I am out there suffering alone with no hope of reprieve.

15. Now that I'm a father, I know that he was trying to help me in his own way, but it wasn't working.

were liberating, and they began the long journey of my healing from a "try harder" mentality to a "trust more" heart.

* * *

"When the *London Times* asked some writers for essays on the topic, 'What's Wrong with the World?' Chesterton sent in the reply shortest and most to the point:

Dear Sirs,

I am.

Sincerely Yours,

G.K. Chesterton."[16]

It's so easy to judge the church with all of her weaknesses. Some people write books about them, making a living by bashing the church, but it is still the bride of Christ, which he laid his life down to save; and in his eyes, she is beautiful! So before you start judging the church (which takes very little intelligence to do, since the flaws are many, and obvious), remember that this is your family too. So grow up, learn some humility, get the "... plank out of your own eye, and then you will see clearly to remove the speck from your brother's eye" (Matt 7:5). The greatest thing that is wrong with the church is you.

* * *

Dietrich Bonheoffer was a pastor during World War II who was martyred in Germany after taking part in an attempt to assassinate Adolf Hitler. Bonheoffer, in his classic work on Christian community, made a profound statement about learning to move past our dreams about the church and loving her:

16. Philip Yancey, *Soul Survivor* (New York, NY: Galilee, 2001).

> God's grace speedily shatters such dreams. Just as surely as God desires to lead us to a knowledge of genuine Christian fellowship, so surely must we be overwhelmed by a great disillusionment with others, with Christians in general, and if we are fortunate, with ourselves.... The sooner this shock of disillusionment comes to an individual and the community the better for both... He who loves his dream of a community more than the Christian community itself becomes a destroyer of the latter, even though his personal intentions may be ever so honest, earnest, and sacrificial.[17]

We can very easily allow our dreams and ideals of what the church "ought to be" get in the way of seeing the beauty that she has, even in all of her ugliness. Just as we learned in the chapter on Ugly Jesus, God hides his beauty in the humanity of the church; flawed, weak humans who make up the church. To the unbelieving eye, the church is an ugly mess; but to Jesus, he sees his bride — and he knows what she will become. Remember that because God wins with an ugly team, he gets all the glory.

Most of our idealism about the church comes from authors that are theoreticians, philosophers, and academics — not practitioners. They are not pastors who live and bleed with the ugly sheep. They don't go down with the ship when tragedy strikes. They keep a comfortable distance, measuring and observing, staying out of the crap that real ministers have to deal with. They are self-proclaimed religious experts who hide behind their education, statistics, and loads of ideas that they could never make happen in a real community of sinful, ugly people. They tell us how weak the church is (like that's a real shock to anyone), and how she ought to do more of this or that. They may be correct, but they miss the point that even in weakness, God's glory shines! They miss The Power of Ugly. Sadly, all this church-bashing is causing a new generation of leaders to attempt to remake the church, trying to

17. Dietrich Bonhoeffer, *Life Together* (San Francisco, CA: Harper San Francisco, 1954), 26-27.

fix it, searching for the best new thing, the "emerging church." Somewhere out there, they think, there's got to be a way to make this ugly thing beautiful. Some, exhausted from trying, have given up altogether, so they just do their own thing with a few select people in a secluded house church.

Our student pastor took a group of his leaders to hear one of these famous Christian authors/theoreticians speak at a fundraising dinner. They had all read his books and were very excited about meeting him and being able to ask him some of the deep questions that they had been chewing on. After the dinner was over and the author was done speaking (a message that everyone in our group, frustratingly, had already heard on-line almost word-for-word), they made their way nervously over to where the man of God was giving autographs. After waiting his turn, the student pastor eagerly began blurting out all his questions about the church and where it was going, things that had been stirred up in him after reading this guy's book. The author, in the middle of signing someone's Bible, looked up at all these young, eager faces, and said, "I don't know what to tell you. I don't work at a church. I've never worked at a church. I am on the road half the time, and I write all my books on solitary retreats. I'm afraid I'm not the guy to be answering these questions." At least he had the humility to tell the truth.[18]

Maybe there are leaders out there who will "emerge" with a new and improved version of the church that is strong and pretty. However, I think that's more likely the "dream of community"

18. Our leaders, needless to say, left frustrated and empty, and our student pastor later told me that from here on out, he would be paying attention to only reading books by people who were actually doing ministry. It's just like the story that John Wimber told of being an eager young Christian and asking his pastor, "When are we really gonna do the stuff that the Bible talks about — like healing people and ministering to the poor?" His pastor replied, "John, we don't really do those things, we just talk about them."

that Bonheoffer warned us about. The reality is probably closer to a line out of one of my favorite movies, *As Good As It Gets*. In the scene, Mr. Neurotic himself, Jack Nicholson,[19] stands up in a psychologist's waiting room filled with broken, desperate people and asked, like an Old Testament prophet, "What if this really is as good as it gets?" Their terrified and hopeless faces said it all. In fact, their expressions looked much like the pastor that wanted to grow his church to 1500 members. What if the church is really as good as she is going to get?

I have often threatened to put an ad in the newspaper advertising the truth about our ugly church. It would just be an honest ad, highlighting some of our weaknesses, with some actual quotes of things people have said about us. It would look something like this:

You are invited to worship with us at the Vineyard

Here is what a few of our guests have said about us:

"We tried to put our baby in the nursery, but no one was there."

"The music was so loud that I had to stuff toilet paper in my ears."

"The sermon was so long that I had to get up three times to pee."

"Someone sitting beside me smelled like they had been drinking and smoking all night." [They probably had been.]

"I'm not sure, but I think one of your members gave me the finger in traffic yesterday." [It was probably the pastor.]

"There was a girl singing on stage and her midriff was showing, and several of the band members were not wearing shoes."

---

19. In reality he probably did very little acting, because in real life he is the part he played in *As Good as it Gets*. I might make a great actor, too, if I could just play myself in every movie I was in.

"The pastor slipped and said a dirty word in his sermon." [At least we hope it was a slip.]

WARNING: this is an Ugly Church! [20]

No perfect people are allowed … you will wreck it!

Here is my point (I know you were beginning to wonder if I had one). I believe, and we are seeing this in our community of faith, that un-churched people are hungry for ugly. They are tired of (and put off by) churches that try to put on a good show to attempt to cover over their ugliness with fig leaves. These people are turned off by churches that present faith as the cure for everything, because they know it's not that easy. They aren't looking for a church that says, "Just fill in the blanks, find the secret knowledge, learn the formulas, and discover your best life now." [21]

As Abigail Van Buren once said, church is not supposed to be, "a museum for saints, but a hospital for sinners." Hospitals are nasty! Life is messy enough on its own; life in community is really messy. It requires huge doses of grace, but that's okay, because that is how Jesus loves his bride. When he pulls a picture of her out of his wallet, it may appear much like the "World's Ugliest Woman," to you, but to him, she is becoming a beautiful bride without a "… stain or wrinkle or any other blemish [ugly], but holy and blameless" (Eph 5:27) to be presented to the one who gave his life for her salvation.

---

20. These weaknesses may seem like they would discourage someone from attending our church, yet in reality, it only scares away the self-righteous. At least, our church is not like a friend of mine's was. He shut down his first church with his last sermon entitled "Five Reasons I Would not go to this church." Phil, I would love to have been there.

21. Pretty churches make it seem like if you start attending, it will be like what they say happens when you play a country song backwards: You get your house back, you get your car back, you get your wife back, and you get your dog back. It's all good!

I love the church, even in her weakness — with her warts and all her uglies. She has been my mother. I am so grateful that I got picked to play on this team. I love being part of the body of Christ — even if it is a flawed and broken group of losers and nobodies just like me. I like the coach the best — he has never lost a game. If you read the end of the Bible, you will see that he transforms this ugly bride into a glorious church filled with his presence (Rev 21:1-5).

The church has loved me, forgiven me, prayed for me, supported me, taught me, wept with me, laughed with me, and formed me into the person that I am becoming. I would have fallen away, given up, and spiritually and perhaps physically died without this community that reflects his beauty through the cracks of their ugliness. People are so isolated and lonely in our supposedly hooked-up, online, connected culture. They're starving for real community. They want to belong. They want to be more than Facebook friends; they want to be loved just as they are. I have found this, and so can you, by being part of an Ugly Church, worshipping a beautiful God.

Our culture is so broken. I want to share something with you, but let me admit right up front that this is a true story that is both sad and tragic — though, in my brokenness, I find it inappropriately humorous. It so clearly reveals our need for community, even if it is ugly. I changed this news story into a top-ten list so that you can review it and discover if you desperately need community like this lady did.[22]

Top Ten Signs That You May Need Community

10. You might need community if your best friend is your pet chimpanzee named Travis.

---

22. Andy Newman, New York Times, http://www.nytimes.com/2009/02/17/world/americas/17iht-chimp.1.20241928.html (accessed September 12, 2010, 2010).

9. You might need community if you bathe with this "pet" named Travis.

8. You might need community in your life if what you look forward to every night is your 300-pound chimp combing your hair.

7. You might need community if Travis sleeps in the same bed as you.

6. You might need community if you like to dress Travis up like a person and then buckle him into the front seat for a drive around town.

5. You might need community if you have to start giving Prozac to your pet Chimp, because he is getting jealous that you have a couple of friends that are humans.

4. You might need community if your pet Chimp attacks your closest human friend in a jealous rage.

3. You might need community in your life if you find yourself struggling with deciding whether to stab Travis with a butcher knife, or to just keep letting him maul your friend.

2. You might need community if you are trying to stop the police from shooting Travis, even after he nearly killed your human friend.

1. You might really need community if you are more distraught over the loss of your pet chimpanzee than you are over your friend who is lying in critical condition in the hospital.

This lady desperately needed community! Any Ugly Church is better than finding community in the arms of a 300-pound Chimpanzee named Travis. God has designed us for community and we need others to become all that he has called us to be. Solitude is great, and I hear God speaking to me through the woods, rocks, trees, and birds — but nothing in all Creation can take the place of face-to-face connection with real people, your family in Christ.

Stop looking for a perfect church — because if you did happen to find one, you would ruin it by joining! Look for an Ugly Church; one that smells, tastes, and feels real. Look for genuine, authentic, broken people who take God very seriously, but do not think they are any big deal. Look for a church that loves the poor and the marginalized. Look for a church that is down to earth, yet reaches upward in worship — one that teaches the Bible in a practical way that helps you grow in your faith. You may find one like this and experience great joy over your discovery — until you get to know the pastor and find out that it is someone just like me! But no matter what, I promise that we will be a better community than Travis can offer.

"Religion [or church] is a big, beautiful, ugly thing," wrote Donald Miller in his book *Searching for God Knows What*. He went on to quote an early church father, Augustine, who said, "The church is a whore and it is my mother." Miller's response to this radical statement was, "…and for reasons I don't understand, Jesus loves the church. And I suppose he loves the church with the same strength of character he displays in his love for me. Sometimes it is difficult to know which is the greater miracle."[23]

As the church lies naked before you, like a whore caught in the very act of adultery — making love to this evil world and cheating on her husband — what do you do? Will you cast the first stone, feeling that you are worthy to be the judge, because you are not guilty of this particular sin? Will you act like Noah's cursed son Ham who stared at his father's nakedness and then went to tell others what he had seen (Gen 9:18-23)? Or will you practice the "backward walk of love" that Ham's two brothers

23. Miller, *Searching for God Knows What*, 212-213.

practiced as they covered the shame of their father's nakedness with a "... love [that] covers a multitude of sins" (1 Pet 4:8)?

We don't have to ask what Jesus would do in this situation; this time he has already shown us: "Husbands, love your wives, just as Christ loved the church and gave himself up for her to make her holy, cleansing her by the washing with water through the word, and to present her to himself as a radiant church, without stain or wrinkle or any blemish, but holy and blameless" (Eph 5:25-27).

Yes, at times, the church is a whore, but she is also my mother who baptized me, welcomed me into God's family, loved me, fed me, cared for me, forgave me, and raised me into the man I am today. The Ugly Church is the soil that God has planted the seed of his kingdom in; and it will grow into a beautiful bride for his glory. So drop your stones, pick up the cross, join an Ugly Church, and learn to start loving what he loves.

Solviture ambulando,
It is solved by walking.
— St. Augustine of Hippo.

Chapter 10. Ugly Altars

Where White Castles Fall

I resent self-help gurus who appear perfect in every way — with their polished white teeth, dark tans, and buns of steel. Though these skinny experts have never struggled with their weight, they love to give advice to the rest of us ugly people on how to be more like them. I guess no one wants to hear a fat guy tell how many times he has tried, failed, and then found that buying bigger pants is just easier.

I also resent stores that have their pant sizes stop at 38, as though no one bigger than that deserves to shop there. Is it me, or are XLs just not what they used to be?[1]

I was shopping in one of those no-size-over-38 stores with my lovely wife a few years ago, when a prissy salesclerk skipped over to me and said with a very non-John-Wayne-sounding voice, "Sir, may I help you?" I said, "Yes. I would like to try these pants on." He then waved his hand in my direction as if to dismiss me and said, "Sir, these are not going to fit you. In fact, nothing we have in this store is going to fit you." I began wondering if God would understand if I "laid hands" on Mr. Prissy and threw him out of the store. Was that wrong? I know that was not very

---

1. It must be some type of an overseas little butt conspiracy where they sit around making those pants, thinking, "these too huge call XL, we call these XXXL."

Christian, especially for a "man of the cloth."

So, biting my tongue so hard that blood ran down both sides of my mouth, I boldly proclaimed, "I will try these pants on." My wife knew I was angry, and that at any cost, I was going to prove a point. In the dressing room, I pulled the pants up and then sucked in with all my might. I was tugging on the zipper like I was at a tractor pull. But they were on, and it didn't matter that the button was about to pop off and possibly kill someone! Just to show him how stupid he was, I proudly walked out of the dressing room like a male model on the runway — except I could not breathe. "Oh no sir, those pants are way too tight," he said, "The zipper is about to burst, and the front pockets are pulling together." My wife tried to help save me, "Honey, they are a little tight." I snapped back, "They fit fine. I'll take them." Of course, they just hung in my closet with the other jeans that I had outgrown years ago.

* * *

"Ladies and gentlemen, this is your pilot speaking…" I never like to hear the pilot's voice on any flight, unless it is after we have landed and he is saying, "Thank you for traveling with us. Have a safe time and enjoy the rest of your trip." Just fly the plane and get us there in one piece.

I had just taken off from the Atlanta airport, after grabbing a tasteless, cold salad with some nasty non-fat dressing. I was trying to be good, since I was on yet another diet. It would be easy to be skinny if I didn't love to eat so much.[2]

The pilot announced, "We are going to have to turn back to

2. In one of my sermons, I joked that I was so large because God had delivered me from anorexia and I was celebrating the victory. After the service a very angry person rebuked me and I know better now. I realize that eating disorders are a horrible problem in our culture and no joking matter.

Atlanta," that information alone would have been bad enough, but he just had to give more details — "One of our engines is not working properly." The plane only had two engines. Why not just turn around and fly back to Atlanta, and land with all of us thinking, "Wow, that was a quick trip," and then give us the bad news? With the announcement came the "spirit of fear," which began working overtime in my mind: *We are never going to make it; this is it! We are going to crash and I'm going to die!* At this point I had to make my seat in the plane into an Ugly Altar, and the plane became my worship cathedral. I made a fresh surrender to God, hoping that he still had plans for me. You can find an altar anywhere if your God does not solely reside in a building that we call a "church."

With my life flashing before me (in my mind I was saying goodbye to my wife and kids), the thought hit me, "Why did I eat that darn, low fat, cold, salad instead of the cheeseburger I really wanted?" It seemed like such a waste to die in a fiery crash with a salad in my stomach as my last meal. Far in the future they will excavate my fossilized remains, and some scientist will falsely declare: "We found a salad eater!" When we made it back to the Atlanta airport safely, I whispered a thank you to Jesus and exited the plane in search of the biggest, greasiest, two-handed burger that I could find in the Atlanta airport.

It didn't take me long — I followed the sweet aroma of sizzling red meat right to a grill with a big fat guy named Bubba behind it — this is always a good sign. You should never trust a skinny guy when he tries to tell you where the best places to eat are. I ordered the *one pounder* with cheese, fries, and a large shake. It was fantastic! I wanted to kiss Bubba. Once we were back on the plane, I unsnapped my too-tight jeans, buckled the seat belt,[3] and

---

3. Thankfully, I did not need to ask for one of those embarrassing belt extenders.

slept like a baby all the way home. I was at peace, ready to meet my Maker, now that I had eaten my Last Supper. If I was going to die, at least I would be happy — a little bigger — but smiling nonetheless, with a little bit of dried chocolate on my goatee and mustard on my shirt. Life is too short to eat tofu and nuts all the time!

*   *   *

I'm all for discipline — trying to take care of our bodies — but not at the expense of living life. Much of our culture's quest for skinny perfection is driven by fear or vanity. Eating healthy is smart, but not when it becomes an obsession rooted in a fear of dying, or a compulsion born out of insecurity. I have found that a far better motive for me to be a good steward of my body is the promise that Jesus gives for our bodies to be resurrected: "…a time is coming and has now come when the dead will hear the voice of the Son of God and those who hear will live" (John 5:25). I believe that this physical body we live in will be remade, renewed, redeemed, restored, and resurrected. When Jesus conquered death, he came out of the grave with the same body that he had walked this earth with earlier, except it was radically transformed by the resurrection. His body was the same, but completely different. He still bore the scars of our salvation, which he shocked "doubting" Thomas with (John 20:20). Even though this new body could walk through walls, the great news was that Jesus could still eat real food! The Scriptures take several opportunities to point out that Jesus ate after the resurrection (Luke 24:30, 24:41-43, and John 21:12-13). O yeah, we will be eating on the new earth and Bubba will be in the kitchen grilling up the one-pounders!

Taking care of our bodies is what N. T. Wright refers to as

"putting up a signpost"[4] that points to what the future holds for us after the resurrection. But what is promised to us is more than just a new body — there is a promise of a new heaven and a new earth (2 Pet 3:13). We do not create our new resurrected body by being good stewards of the ones we inhabit here on earth, but we put a sign in the ground that points to what the future will bring when Christ returns. The same principle holds true for our responsibility to tend the garden (Gen 2:15). When we fulfill the command in Genesis to take care of this planet, we are planting a signpost in the ground, pointing to God's plans to completely remake this planet into a new earth.

This concept of putting up a signpost is also a reason why we should work for justice now. We know we will never establish heaven on earth, but we still must proclaim that a king is coming with scales in his hands to measure out justice for all. Every act, no matter how small, of kindness, forgiveness, working for justice, or even recycling acts as a signpost pointing to the promise of God's new creation, which will come in the return of Jesus and the resurrection.

Some say that all of this is like polishing the brass on the Titanic. It is a waste of time because it is all going to sink. They say that all we need to do is try to get a few more people saved, because Armageddon is coming, so hunker down and pray for the Rapture. This narrow-minded, escapist view leaves the church powerless to make a difference in this world. It robs the church of any hope of fulfilling its mission to see God's kingdom spread throughout the whole world, offering a better future.

The message of the gospel is so much larger than just getting someone to heaven. We have a promise that our "... labor in the Lord is not in vain" (1 Cor 15:58). This promise is anchored in the

---

4. Wright, *Surprised by Hope*.

hope of our resurrection, which was made certain to us through the testimony of Jesus' resurrection. In his resurrection, we have hope that every seed we plant in his name will bear fruit for all of eternity. We can know that every sacrifice of dying to something — on whatever kind of cross or Ugly Altar — will end in resurrection.

This was the hope that sustained Abraham as he laid his son Isaac on an Ugly Altar of stones. With tears running down his wrinkled face, he drew back the knife — having already died to his son in his heart, when the Angel of God said, "Stop!" The only way Abraham could obey God's call for ultimate sacrifice was because he had faith in the resurrection (Heb 11:19).

The sacrifice of taking care of my body is not for the vain pleasure of pulling off my shirt to impress the ladies, and it isn't some fearful attempt to hold off death as long as possible. What we are engaged in doing is what author Eugene Peterson called, "the practice of resurrection."[5] This practice is learning to work in his power through the Holy Spirit. So we work now, pointing to a better future. We are not earning or creating this new body or the new heavens and the new earth; we are only witnessing to the truth that it is coming.

This new creation, which has already begun, will be completed when God makes his new heaven and new earth. He will resurrect us to live in that new world. This is so much more than just going to heaven — it is a hope that connects all we love and do now to the future. My little buddy, Sunday, our fourteen year-old golden retriever that I had to put down, will be waiting for me to throw the ball so he can (sometimes) retrieve it on the new soil of the restored planet earth. This restored planet will never be soaked with blood, pollution, or tears. We are to be shaped here and now by this hope in the future, which Jesus has promised. We begin now to

---

5. Peterson, *Living the Resurrection*, 75.

practice resurrection; building for the future by sharing and living the good news among those trapped in darkness, fear, emptiness, and hopelessness.[6]

The promise of new creation is that through the resurrection God will transform not just our bodies, but our entire beings to fully reflect his beauty. This hope gives us confidence that what God has begun in our lives, transforming our ugliness into beauty, will be completed at the resurrection. "... But we know that when he appears, we shall be *like him,* for we shall see him as he is. Everyone who has *this hope* in him purifies himself, just as he is pure" (1 John 3:2-3, emphasis added). Because we have this hope to be like Jesus, we can begin to practice resurrection by growing in his likeness — not to earn it or create it, but to walk in the promise of it.

* * *

On this journey of growing into his likeness, there will be lots of stumbles, setbacks, failures, and false starts, which will lead to many opportunities to practice dying on Ugly Altars. We will never arrive at perfection — it will take the resurrection to get us where we are destined to be. Often, just when we start seeing some real progress in our spiritual growth, seeds of pride begin to sprout, telling us lies: *Wow, I am so disciplined. Look at how faithful I have been. I have become so humble and loving. Why can't others be as committed as I am? You need to show them how it is done; yes, that must be my calling.* But, of course, always giving all the glory to God for *my* great victories.

Religious pride is such a trap: being humble, and yet so proud of it. It is deceptive and difficult to detect. It is like trying to smell your own breath. It takes a true friend to tell you when your breath

---

6. For more information about this topic, see Peterson's *Living the Resurrection* and Wright's *Surprised by Hope.*

smells like you have been eating a crap sandwich. In our culture, however, self-confidence, success, and accomplishment in our own strengths are considered things to be bragged about; but to God, it all stinks.

Those of us who feel like we have made great progress in our spirituality easily become religious prostitutes, selling our secrets to those willing to pay: *I have the secret knowledge for how you can be happy, thin, healthy, beautiful, and even holy — let me show you how I got here.* This is worship on the pretty altar of human pride that the prophet Ezekiel warned about, "You trusted in your beauty and used your fame to become a prostitute" (Ezek 16:15).

One thing that I know for sure is that God is relentless in exposing arrogant, self-confident pride in those he loves.[7] He is really good at humbling the proud. And when God lifts our skirts to expose our nakedness, it is a mercy killing. When he pulls out the knife to stab our self-confidence to death, or just raises up a little sprinkler to bring us down, he shows no mercy. Don't believe those ten-cent religious lies people throw around: *God will never embarrass you. God will never give you more than you can handle. God will never hurt you.* We say those things because we think we want a gentle, tame, and safe God whom we can control and who understands and approves of our pride. However, he loves us way too much to leave us to ourselves. He has shown me over and over that it is never about Jamie's strength. In fact, all of my strength must die on Ugly Altars before I will experience the grace of resurrection.

* * *

I'm no big deal to my church; they have seen plenty of my uglies. It is healthy for me to stay surrounded by a bunch of Carls —

---

7. He is far more concerned with these things than the outward, surface-level sins that we tend to judge others by.

people to whom I am no big deal. They are not afraid to tell me the truth, even when it hurts, and they will hold my hand when I am lost, helping me find the way out of Fort Wilderness. In addition to the church that I am a part of, I have the gift of getting together every week with a group of pastors in our city. I call this small group my "Monday Morning Pastor Buddies," and they are the ones who have helped to keep me somewhat sane and still in the ministry. We have met together for almost fourteen years now, every Monday, for three hours. We laugh, cry, tell stories, pray, eat, and most of all, act like Carls to each other. I want to say thanks to my Monday Morning Pastor Buddies: Dennis, Jorge, David, Jeff, David, and Bob for loving, challenging, teaching, and protecting me from me.[8]

It's a little easier to stay grounded when you are at home, where everyone knows the real you. But there is some kind of magic that happens to pastors when we travel away from home to minister. We almost instantly become the experts! We are the anointed men of God with all the answers. One time, as much as I did not want this to happen, I succumbed to these lies as they crept into my heart. I was speaking in a large church in Indiana and the Lord was showing up and people were being deeply touched by God. They were singing my praises, and I was soaking it up, oh yeah, and always giving all the glory to God, of course. I was sharing with the church some of my recent victories, which included having lost some weight and finding the secret for my new strength. I offered them these "Secrets to your Best Life Now," telling them that by following my example and applying my keys to success,

---

8. Thanks for loving me through all of these years, guys — you are one ugly group, and that is why I fit in so well. I promise not to tell which one of you is claiming the promise of Ezekiel 23:20.

they could become just like me!

After the service that night, I felt exceptionally victorious and thought I was well deserving of a reward. So we stopped at a White Castle and I bought a bag of those little burgers. These things are like grease pellets — but they taste wonderful! We don't have White Castles in Florida, so it is a rare treat for me to dine there. I was staying at a friend's beautiful home in a historic neighborhood,[9] and we went back to his house to eat. My hosts and my wife went to bed, leaving me alone with the whole bag of White Castle burgers! I stayed up and proceeded to pound down the entire bag of grease pellets.

Of course, after eating all of those burgers, I needed something sweet; something like cookies and milk. I hadn't splurged in weeks, and I thought that I deserved this. I love dunking cookies — I am very good at it after years of practice.[10] So, that night I settled for a bag of Chips Ahoy with a large glass of milk. I went to bed stuffed and slept like a baby.

I awoke in the morning and made the recommitment to get back on the wagon. I had my normal breakfast — 100% bran cereal with skim milk and bananas, and some coffee. (Can you smell disaster coming?) "Honey, I am going for a power walk," were my last words to my wife. I set out to atone for my sinful indulgence the night before. I had my Nikes on with my white daisy duke gym shorts. I was looking good — power-walking through this multi-million dollar neighborhood with yards that looked like manicured mini parks and homes like the ones that you only see in magazines. I was revisiting some

---

9. This friend is the leading cardiologist in the city, so when I say beautiful and historic; I mean it!

10. My wife has been trying to kill me slowly over the years by baking the world's best chocolate chip cookies.

of the previous night's victories, and trying to figure out how I was going to follow up such a powerful message with an even greater home run tonight.

I was about a mile into the walk when a noise came out of me that sounded like the gurgling noise in Harry's stomach in the classic comedy *Dumb and Dumber*. (You know, the scene where he uses his date's bathroom, but then finds out that the toilet does not work.) Then it hit me like an epiphany: White Castle burgers + bag of cookies + milk + 100% bran cereal + banana + coffee = "Oh. God! Oh, God! Oh, God! Help!" I quickly turned, heading back to my friend's house as I began violently cramping.[11] I was beginning to lose control, and I was nowhere near my increasingly crucial destination.

This is when "great faith" makes a difference in our lives. I began to pray for God's strength, groaning out the promise, "I can do everything through him who gives me strength" (Phil 4:13).[12] Well, prayer and scripture promises were not working. I began to waddle like Charlie Chaplin. I was taking little baby steps, squeezing my cheeks together with all my might.

In crisis mode, I quickly assessed my options: #1. Make it back to the house. *That will never happen.* #2. Waddle up to a stranger's house and ask to defile their beautiful marble bathroom. *No, they may not be home, and they could have a vicious guard dog.* #3. Find a bush. This looked like the only plan that would work. Moses may have found God in a burning bush and then taken off his shoes; but my experience was going to

---

11. Why is it that the closer that we get to the finish line, the more we lose our ability to control things? When I have to pee, I am in complete control, until I get within sight of the finish line; then I begin to leak.

12. It worked for Tim Tebow who wore this Scripture under his eyes and then won the College Football National Championship for the Florida Gators (I just threw that in for my Ohio friends!)

involve taking off my shorts in broad daylight! Why me, God? What have I ever done to deserve this? "Eat White Castle, bran, and minister in pride," seemed to be the answer from God.

The harder I squeezed and the faster I tried to move, the more my bowels began to release.[13] It was coming out, whether I liked it or not. I quickly searched for a place to practice dying. Where would I find my Ugly Altar? There it was! It was just off the road, in front of a beautiful yard with a tree large enough to cover me (at least from one direction). Before I could even fully pull down my white gym shorts, I erupted. It was an explosion — a rectum rocket! How humiliating — being there in broad daylight; the "man of God" with his naked butt exposed to the world. I had struck another sprinkler, only this time it was both painful and nasty. I will spare you a description of all of the sounds, smells, and colors, but let me just say, it was ugly![14]

Dogs barked and cars drove by as I quickly pulled up my gym shorts (which were half full) and then began walking back like a three-year-old in a dirty diaper! Each step of the journey home was painful and humiliating. I waddled to the house, snuck in through the back door, and headed to our bedroom. I began to whisper cries of help to my wife as I ran into the bathroom. With loving concern, she asked what was wrong, and then she took one look at me, lost all compassion, and

---

13. In a moment like this, you could easily fall in the trap of "just letting off a little pressure." No way! It's like an avalanche that just starts with one too many snowflakes — you don't want to go that direction!

14. Eric W. Gritsch, *The Wit of Martin Luther* (Minneapolis, MN: Fortress Press, 2008), 97. Martin Luther publicly chastised people in his sermons if they defecated in public. He would refer to them as "diabolically shameless." Gratefully he was not pastoring in Indiana.

screamed, "Oh, my God! What have you done! You're dripping everywhere!"

Kim came to my rescue, as she has many times in the past. She helped me clean up as only a loving wife could do. She has been helping me clean up my messes for over thirty years — which has been her way of practicing dying.[15]

Now we had to make a hard decision — to come clean and confess, or wait for one of the doctor's neighbors to call him and report that they saw a pervert defile their yard and then enter his house. I came clean to them, and after a great laugh, they practiced the backward walk of love, forgiving me and covering my...well, you know. After much reflection, the only thing that I see that was in sinful violation of the Scriptures was that I never went back and buried my poop.[16]

Times of humiliation like this help soften our hearts for others who suffer similar experiences. I felt great compassion as I read this article:

81-Year-Old Woman Arrested for Urinating in a Park

Prosecutors asked a judge to throw out a public lewdness charge against an 81-year-old woman accused of urinating in a public park when she couldn't make it to the bathroom, the city attorney said Thursday. Municipal prosecutors in Mobile filed a motion Wednesday to drop the charge against Lula Mae Battle, who suffers from incontinence. Her arrest sparked calls from upset city residents. "As far as

---

15. There will be crowns for her in heaven (see *Ugly Marriage*, Chapter 14).

16. In Deuteronomy 23:13 (NIV), the people of God were told, "When you relieve yourself, dig a hole and cover up your excrement." The main reason, I believe, was so that the Lord wouldn't step in it as he walked around the camp! Check it out if you do not believe me. I love the rawness and practicality of the Ugly Bible.

we're concerned this is over," said city attorney Larry Wettermark ... [17]

"Thank you, Jesus. Glory, Hallelujah!" Battle told the Press-Register newspaper after learning of the city's motion.[18]

I celebrate with you Lula Mae!

To this day, my friends in Indiana swear that the tree that I made into an Ugly Altar is now the tallest tree in the neighborhood. Apparently, humility makes good fertilizer! I will not disclose the name of this doctor to protect what remains of his dignity in the community, but his initials are Dr. B. S.!

17. Do not attempt to say that name slowly.

18. "81-Year-Old Woman Arrested For Urinating In A Park," News One, http://newsone.com/nation/news-one-staff/81-year-old-woman-arrested-for-urinating-in-a-park/ (accessed September 12, 2010).

You can safely assume you've created God
in your own image when it turns out
that God hates all the same people you do.
— Anne Lamott

Chapter 11. Ugly Mystic

I Hear Voices

I am jealous of the titles that other faiths have for their spiritual leaders. As Christians we have reverend, doctor, bishop, apostle, pastor, and my personal favorite, clergy. Clergy sounds like something we tried to avoid back in the '70s. These names sound professional, but they do not make you think of a mystic or a holy man. The best Christian title that I can come up with is minister. The problem with that term is that in the Bible, minister is always a verb and never a noun. It is not a title that you carry, but something that you do, something that every Christian is called to do. Except that many church leaders today have embraced the concept of being the CEO of the church, riding high as the head rancher.

Why do all the other faiths have such cool names for their holy men and women? I want to be Rabbi Jamie, Jamie the Imam, Guru Jamie, Maharishi Jamie, Zen Master Jamie, Shaman Stilson or Medicine Man Jamie. But I guess it makes no difference what people call me — it's who I am and how I live that will define me. I don't want to wear some religious title that makes me *sound* holy; I want to *be* a spiritual person — an Ugly Mystic — someone who knows his God personally.

What is an Ugly Mystic, you ask? I'm not sure, but it sounds... mystical. Throughout church history those who were called mystics were weird, eccentric, out-there people — that's me! But most mystics were extremely disciplined individuals who spent lots of time in solitude, fasting, praying, meditating, and being silent for long hours — that's not me!

When I try to read most of these mystic authors, they are so mystical that I cannot understand much of what they are saying. Their approach is so deep that it is over my head. They set such a high bar for what it takes to be holy that I give up before I even start. It is like a marathon runner who has been in training for years inviting you to join them on a twenty mile run — but you get out of breath just walking up the stairs. Many mystics tend to fall into the trap of finding the secret to everything inside themselves. They either make God into a transcendent genie that gives them whatever they wish for or into an impersonal force like in *Star Wars*. They speak of tapping into the cosmic energy, the law of attraction, finding the god inside you, and harnessing the creative powers of the universe.

Some of this kind of mystical thinking can be found in the bestselling book, *The Secret*. This is just a re-branded form of Gnosticism mixed with Pantheism in which god is in everything and everything is god. The problem with this is that the God of the Bible, the God revealed to us through Jesus, is not equal to, or limited by creation, because he "... created all things, and by ...[his] will they were created ... " (Rev 4:11). He is the Creator and stands as Lord over all of creation.

The God of the universe cannot be tapped into or manipulated by our own human efforts. As the Scriptures say, he "... lives in unapproachable light, ... " (1 Tim 6:16).[1] Throughout the

---

1. Think of one of the animated movies where a bug is captured by the overwhelming beauty of the bright light and is blinded by all its glory. Screaming in sheer ecstasy, he flies toward the light, only to get zapped!

Bible people paid dearly for thinking God could be treated or worshipped however they chose. I am reminded of two priests' kids who had grown up around the things of God. They had fallen into the religious trap of familiarity with God, and lost their respect for him. Bored with always doing things the way that God had commanded, they decided to make up their own mixture of incense. They began offering to God what they chose, and not what he required. They became the offering when they were burned up in a ball of fire from the presence of God (Lev 10:1-2).

* * *

If we desire to become Ugly Mystics who seek after the true God, we must keep in mind that he is an unpredictable, incomprehensible, and unapproachable Holy God. Keep that in mind as you hear stories of people who have near-death experiences and see a safe, warm, inviting light that seems to remove all their fear of dying. Beware, because Satan is an expert mystic — he can even be "... transformed into an angel of light" (2 Cor 11:14, KJV). Satan loves to give people false peace, removing fears through lies similar to the very first falsehood recorded in Scripture. He lied to Adam and Eve, telling them, "You will not surely die,..." (Gen 3:4). This lie gave them the false assurance that they could disobey God without consequences.

Satan is the inventor of religions and the author of alternatives to true worship. He does not care if you worship a toad, a tree, a cross, a book, a holy person, a fat bald-headed guy sitting in a very uncomfortable position, or a picture of your favorite televangelist that cries for you. Anything, anyone, anyway ... except Jesus.

Jesus warned us of trying to enter into his "sheep pen... some other way," (John 10). He tells us that he is the only door to God, and only through him can you enter into God's flock. He is both the shepherd who leads his sheep, calling them by name, and the door that they must walk through in order to enter his flock. Jesus warns us of the thief that attempts to imitate the voice of the shepherd in order to "... steal and kill and destroy;... " the sheep (John 10:10). Jesus, while talking about the thief, says that his "sheep [do] not listen to [him]." Learning to hear the voice of the shepherd is essential for the health and safety of the sheep.

If you want to be an Ugly Mystic like I do, then you must learn to recognize the voice of the shepherd. When the thief dresses up as the shepherd, do as Jenny said, "Run, Forrest, run!" We must remember that all that shines is not gold, and all of the voices that are speaking are not God's. If you want to become an Ugly Mystic, there will be many voices inviting you to listen, but there is only one voice that wants to "give you life more abundantly." All the rest want to "steal, kill, and destroy" your relationship with Jesus.

* * *

Why is it that so many followers of Jesus think that being spiritual means you have to be weird? It seems that the stranger you act and the louder you say religious things, the more spiritual people think you are. This kind of thing makes me want to only hang out with lost people. At least lost people are real, and often more spiritual than those running around doing weird stuff and calling themselves Christians. I can't tell you how many sincere people I have dealt with over the years who felt that they had heard the voice of God telling them to do stupid, painful, and at times, evil things. Here are a few sad examples of people who set out to be mystics, to be open to hear voices and insights from the spiritual world, only to end up in a horrible mess.

After a small group Bible study, one of our young ladies informed us that she was going to marry Don Johnson.[2] Let me just say that this girl was no beauty queen. But no amount of reasoning could stop her from quitting her job and moving to Miami to follow the "voice of God" into Don's loving arms. What she needed at that moment was a Simon Cowell to burst her bubble and tell her the truth. "Honey, I don't know what voice you are listening to, but it isn't God. You are deceived and delusional. You are overweight and unattractive, and you have absolutely no chance of marrying Don." I chickened out, thinking, maybe it was God telling her to marry him. And why waste the time, since she had already made up her mind.

Any pastor's advice can always be trumped by throwing the "I heard God tell me to do this" card down on the table. That's the point where I walk away from the conversation, because who wants to argue with God? This is why it is so important when you are asking for advice and counsel from your spiritual leaders to say things like: "This is what I think I heard," or "I'm not sure if it was me just wanting to hear this or God said it to me." This attitude leaves lots of room for being wrong and allows you to be open to wise counsel.

One of the saddest stories involves a guy that I will call Freddy. Freddy was part of our church and had started coming to me for counseling because his wife had caught him in adultery. Now they were separated, and he was a broken man who desperately wanted his wife back. He began spending a large amount of time praying and reading the Bible, asking God what to do. Then, Freddy heard a voice answer him, but he neglected to share it with me or anyone else. The truth was that the pimple-faced bag boy at Publix could have told him that he was missing God. Why is it that when it comes

---

2. At this time, *Miami Vice* was at its peak and he was one of the hottest hunks in Hollywood.

to the most important decisions, Christians often act on their own and violate the Biblical warning that there is wisdom in many wise counselors? Hearing voices alone — disconnected from a spiritual community, with no accountability — is spiritual suicide.

I knew something was wrong the moment I saw Freddy walk into my office with his hand completely bandaged. When I asked him what had happened, he told me that he had been feeling very guilty for what he had done. He said, "Jamie, God told me to show my wife how sorry I was for hurting her by cutting off my ring finger. So when I was at work [Freddy was a chef], I took a sharp knife, and chopped it off!" I almost threw up.

He went on to share that he had placed his detached finger in some meat wrapping paper and sent it to his wife as a peace offering, with a note signed, "Love, Freddy."

Now, as he was weeping in my office, he could not understand why his wife had filed for a divorce and taken a restraining order out against him! At this point I snapped and became Pastor Simon Cowell, screaming at Freddy, "You are an idiot. That was not God who told you to do that, it was the devil." Counseling has never been my strong point. What I actually wanted to tell Freddy was that if he was trying to reach his wife's heart, he had cut off the wrong appendage!

These may seem like obvious deceptions to you, but there are far more subtle ones. We have an enemy who is really good at deceiving people. He makes evil look good and good look evil. If we want to be Ugly Mystics and learn to listen to God, our protection from being deceived is to practice what I call *Safe Listening*. We need to put on the proper protection before we attempt to penetrate the spiritual realm and look for the spiritual intimacy of listening for God's voice. This way, the "God told me to …" excuse does not give us license to just do whatever we want.

If you want to be an Ugly Mystic and hear God talk to you, here are a couple of Safe Listening principles:

First, God will never tell you to do something that violates his word. If what you are hearing contradicts Scripture, submit to God's written word.

Second, if you receive an impression that you feel is from God and it is of a serious nature — like something life-changing or dangerous — share what you feel you heard with a trusted spiritual advisor (or at least the bag boy at Publix). Seek wise, mature, godly counsel.

Third, remember most of what you will ever hear from the heavenly Father is encouragement. The Father delights in telling us over and over how much he loves us. If what you hear is so good that you feel unworthy to hear it, then that is a great sign that you are listening to the voice of God.

Fourth, God loves to talk about practical things. He loves to tell me how I can be nicer to my wife. He will often remind me of people who need to be prayed for. He has suggested that I go mow someone's lawn, write a note of encouragement, phone a friend, or take a walk. God likes practical mystics. It is not very often that God will speak to us about the mysteries of the universe, or who the antichrist will be, or when the end of the world will come. But, he will talk to us about our pride, bitterness, impatience, and unloving attitude. He will usually ask us to do simple childlike things that can be accomplished that day.[3]

Jesus taught his disciples that a truly spiritual person would be more like a little child (Matt 18:1-4). He was not encouraging

---

3. Some examples could be: "Go wash the dishes for your wife." "Call your friend who you know needs some encouragement." "Turn off the TV and spend some time in my word." "Let's go for a walk and talk."

us to act immaturely — to start sucking our thumbs and shoving crayons up our noses. Jesus appealed to the humility, simplicity, honesty, and trusting heart that a child has. The sad thing about our culture is that as we grow older, we forget all the wonderful qualities of childlikeness. Instead, we bring with us all of the immature and selfish attitudes of childhood into adulthood. We pout, throw temper tantrums, grip our stuff in selfishness, avoid responsibility, expect the world to revolve around us, and even mess our britches. The truly spiritual person, the mystic, is childlike in all the positive ways that Jesus described.

Jesus loved children, and they loved him. Children loved Jesus because he was so childlike. Jesus laughed with and played with the children just like one of them. Children will tell you who the spiritual people are by who they are drawn to. An uptight, judgmental, joyless, Bible scholar — a person who is against more than they are for — will never have children drawn to them. Whatever a mystic is or does, they must always reflect the character of childlikeness, which is what Jesus refers to as "kingdom greatness."

* * *

I write the impressions I receive from the Father in my journal. I do what we teach beginning Ugly Mystics to do — give expressions to our impressions. This simply means to write down what we feel the Father is saying to us. I like to read some verses out of the Bible and listen for his living voice to speak to me through his written Word.[4] Your journal is not a diary; it is your history with God. I will put it into context with what may be happening in my life by writing some brief details like, "I feel like

---

4. Old Mystics called this Lectio Divina — which means "spiritual reading."

quitting today, tired of Christians, they are never happy, always judging, complaining and never listening to anything I try to teach them."

Here is an example of one of my journal pages:

July 25

Yes to Total Trust

Up early and I can't sleep struggling with how to overcome our financial woes.

"I have trusted in the Lord without wavering"
Psalms 26:1

Father, how I wish this was true, for I have often found myself in fear, worry and striving from not trusting. Help me be a better truster and less of a trier.

"Jamie, your gift of trust to me is the highest act of love in worship. To put your trust in me is to stop depending on anything else. There is always a No to saying Yes to trusting me. No to relying on yourself. No to looking to others. One Yes to me will cost you many No's to others. I receive your trust as worship — for it is surrender to me, honor to me, and faith in me. To trust in me with all your heart is to love me with all your heart.

"My son, I invite you into the place of joy and peace through the door of trust — rely on me, depend on me, rest in me, and receive from me. Trust me to the end, finding me waiting to receive you with my 'well done good and faithful servant.'"

Father, I say Yes, to total trust in you for perfect peace.

There is no one set way to do this, so find a form that works for you. You will notice that I put my name before writing what I feel the Father is saying to me so it is personal. This is important because it is not just a teaching or collection of good thoughts; it is a loving impression for Jamie from my Shepherd who "calls his own sheep by name" (John 10:3).

As you learn to pay attention to these impressions from God, you will discover that he can speak to you through just about anything. Dreams can be a powerful way for God to communicate with us. If a dream seems to be a God dream, I write it in my journal. Sometimes dreams are just from eating too much pizza — those are what I call "flushers," and they are not worth recording. Some dreams may be nightmares that come from the enemy, and after those, you need to ask the Lord to cleanse them from your mind.

Discernment comes with practice. We begin learning the characteristics of the Shepherd's voice. His voice is usually only a still small voice, and he rarely shouts. Be careful, because doubt can easily rob you from hearing him by telling you that it was "just you hearing what you wanted to hear." He whispers because he wants us to seek out his voice, which requires us to quiet ourselves and listen for him. We will seldom hear God when we are in a hurry (except to hear him say, "Slow down"). It takes time to have quality communication, whether in a marriage or in our spiritual lives. Love requires time, attention, and focus.

God speaks to me through movies, art, birds, trees, and he has even spoken to me through rocks! I love rocks. Out of all things in creation that he could choose to compare himself to, God often chooses a rock (Gen 49:24, Deut 32:4, 2 Sam 22:32, and many more). I love to sit on a large rock and let it talk to me about what the creator is like. John Calvin once called creation "God's second Bible." That is so true, and I love to read the words God has written in a flower, through a sunset, or in the roar of a waterfall.[5]

---

5. Peter Brown, *Augustine of Hippo* (Los Angeles, CA: University of California Press, 2000), 101. One of the greatest thinkers and theologians the

Most people that I know suffer from a disease called Nature Deficit Disorder.[6] NDD is a result of our hurried lifestyles combined with too much television, movies, computers, and noise. We can choose to fight NDD by unplugging our electric diversions and plugging into the rhythms of God's creation.

There is a certain place that I love to walk to in the Northeast Georgia Mountains. I call it the "Council of the Elders," and it is full of old Ugly Mystics that have stood the test of time. These elders are giant, old trees that have weathered storms, depressions, wars, and generations of people who have stood before them. They have been elders to me, giving me honest and wise counsel.[7] They are covered with scars from many battles — they wear them as badges of honor that tell their stories. Trees, like rocks, are just window dressing to many people who are blind to their majesty. Eugene Petersons wrote, "A bad person doesn't see the same tree that a good person sees. A bad life incapacitates us for real life."[8] Jesus said it this way, "Blessed are the pure in heart, for they will see God" (Matt 5:8). This seeing includes being able to see the true of beauty of all that God has made.

Elizabeth Barrett Browning had eyes to see this beauty, and wrote, "Earth's crammed with Heaven, and every common bush afire with

church has ever known, St Augustine, was converted by hearing the voice of God speak to him through the words of a child singing, "take it and read, take it and read." He received this as a divine command to open the scriptures and read whatever his eyes saw first. Who knows, it may have been a verse 17.

6. Richard Louv, *Last Child in the Woods: Saving Our Children From Nature-Deficit Disorder* (Chapel Hill, NC: Algonquin Books, 2008).

7. On a recent visit to "the Council of the Elders" with several of my grandchildren, we paused to let the Lord speak to us through elders. My 10-year-old grandson, Riley, heard one of the elders encourage him that there are many great adventures ahead as he follows Jesus.

8. Eugene Peterson, *Leap Over a Wall: Earthy Spirituality for Everyday Christians* (New York, NY: Harper Collins, 1998), 212.

God; but only he who sees, takes off his shoes, the rest sit round it, and pluck the black berries."[9] Take a walk out into God's creation and truly see a bush, a tree, or a rock. Take off your shoes because you will be on holy ground. Listen for the voice of God. Watch for the fire of his beauty that fills his creation.

I was once performing a wedding on the beach when a young boy picking up seashells interrupted me. He was shocked to see a religious ceremony outside the four walls of a church building. He blurted out, "You can't have a wedding out here — this isn't a church!"

I could have just ignored the little blessing, but I seized the opportunity as a teachable moment. Stopping the ceremony, I asked him, "Who do you think made this beach we are standing on?" He replied with some embarrassment, "God did." I said, "You're right! He loves all that he has created, and he does not just live in a little building we call a church. He is so big that he fills the entire universe, so he is here just as much as inside any building. So scram you little jerk before I whip your rude little butt." Okay, I didn't say the last part; I did think it though. Was that wrong?

An Ugly Mystic sees God *everywhere* and listens for God in *everything*, and worships God *anywhere*. Ugly Mystics are just spiritual beggars who hunger for more of God wherever they can find him. They are people who have been "ruined" by having tasted of the goodness of the Lord and because now nothing else satisfies.

Ugly Mystics learn to hear God even in non-Christian movies, books, and unbelieving artists who are just singing about life. My wife heard God speak to her out of a line of a movie that we had watched several times before — *As Good As It Gets*. Jack Nicholson's character tells his waitress, "I might be the only person on the face

---

9. Elizabeth Barrett Browning, *Aurora Leigh* (London: J. Miller, 1864), Book VII.

of the earth that knows you're the greatest woman on earth. I might be the only one who appreciates how amazing you are in every single thing that you do..." As Kim was spending some time just listening to God, she heard the Father use these words out of this worldly movie telling her, "I get it about you." These simple words coming from the lips of God as he was speaking to one of his daughters was life to Kim.

Some will choke on the thought of God speaking to us through someone like Jack Nicholson, yet in the Bible, God spoke through a donkey to rebuke one of his prophets.[10] Anything or anyone can be a mouthpiece for God; we just need to be open to listening. Once we open our hearts to accept the truth that God loves to communicate with us through more ways than we could ever imagine, we can begin to become Ugly Mystics. Ugly Mystics discover how to hear the inaudible, see the invisible, know the unknowable, and experience the unexplainable. This doesn't happen by sitting in some lotus position, eating tofu and nuts, shut away in some monastery, and it doesn't happen by putting on a display of piety at church every Sunday. It happens when normal, down-to-earth people live out their lives with Jesus in the midst of a loud and busy world. In fact, the more spiritual we become, the more human we will act. The most spiritually mature mystics that I have ever met are humble, normal people. They are not scary weirdoes that you would never want to go to the movies with.

We live in a world that is starving for God. There is a longing for transcendence and spiritual fulfillment, a sense that there has to be more to life. People search for it in money, pleasures, addictions, and any kind of thrill. They hope that these things will

---

10. We will talk more about this donkey in the next chapter on *Ugly Preaching*.

help to bring them back to life. It has been said that, "The young man who rings the bell at the brothel is unconsciously looking for God."[11]

The Apostle Paul once quoted one of the popular pagan poets of his day who wrote, "In him we live and move and have our being"(Acts 17:28). This poem was written about the mythological god, Zeus, but Paul lifted this nugget of truth out of the hands of those who did not know the true God and interpreted their own writings for them. In doing this, he revealed the living God to them in a new way — and from their own words! This is what we must do as Ugly Mystics — help our culture discover the truth of God hidden in every common bush.

Movies, rap, the bag boy, even country music, and especially children can all be voices of God for Ugly Mystics. Are you listening for the Shepherd's voice? I hope you will find a journal and a Bible and then go find a rock to sit on, go to the beach, or flop down on your toilet and learn to be an Ugly Mystic — a normal, earthy, childlike human who is hungry for the voice of God wherever you can find it. Or you could just go rent *As Good As It Gets* or *Forrest Gump* or *Gran Torino* and listen for the voice of the Father to speak to you. You will be on your way to becoming an Ugly Mystic. "... Man does not live on bread alone, but on every word that comes from the mouth of God" (Matt 4:4).

---

11. Bruce Smith, *The World, The Flesh, and Father Smith*, Houghton Mifflin (Boston, MA: 1945). This quote is also often attributed to G. K. Chesterton.

I preach as though ne'er to preach again;
as a dying man to dying men.
— Richard Baxter

Chapter 12. Ugly Preaching

The Ass of God

When I first made the Ugly Exchange, giving my heart to Jesus, I spent a lot of time preaching in the woods. I would preach to the birds, squirrels, and cows.[1] My first pastor was named Lou, and he pastored a little Pentecostal church with maybe twenty-five people on a good week — and I brought half of those people with me! Lou's church was in a little town in Florida called Lu Lu,[2] and this little Ugly Church opened its arms to welcome this hippie on probation, that had just given his life to Jesus.

One day in 1976, I went with Pastor Lou and my friend Bill in his 1972 VW Beetle to go visit someone in a hospital. As we were traveling back, Pastor Lou, out of nowhere, reached down, picked up his King James Bible, handed it to me, and said, "Here, Jamie. Preach us a message." I was shocked! How did he know that I wrestled every day with wanting to become a preacher? Did he know that I felt so unqualified and unworthy? Did those cows tell on me? No, Pastor Lou was just doing what a kingdom leader does — they call out the destiny they discern in others.[3]

---

1. Actually, they were better listeners than most church people!

2. I hear the Father laughing!

3. This has been one of my primary missions over the years with young

I finally had the chance to preach an official sermon — with real people listening! My strategy has always been ready-shoot-aim, so without thinking, I said, "Sure, but what scripture should I use?" Pastor Lou had no formal training as a pastor; he would just smell out the texts that he would preach on, so he didn't give me any help.[4] I opened the Bible randomly and looked for verse 17 (a technique theologians call the "Hunt and Dip Method"), and then preached on it for about twelve minutes. I have no idea what I said, but I am sure it was deep and profound ... *not!*

Can someone preach without proper training? In the seventeenth century, the "Pharisees" of the day would put preachers who didn't have the proper credentials in jail just to keep them quiet. One of the guys that they did this to wrote a book called *The Pilgrim's Progress* while he was in imprisoned.[5]

Jesus' disciples blew the minds of the trained religious experts of the time when they spoke with wisdom and authority about the Scriptures. They were just common and uneducated fishermen, ugly to the eyes of the religious professionals. In an attempt to condemn these Ugly Preachers for preaching the message of Jesus, the religious leaders called them "... unschooled, ordinary

---

people. I look to see leadership in them and then call them out. Just as I needed someone to believe in me, there is a whole generation of fatherless kids just waiting to be called out to be the next: Caleb, Jael, Debra, Joseph, Daniel, Josiah, Esther and Mary — all under twenty-one when God used them to change the world!

4. He would read until he smelled the roses, and that became his text to preach on. To a hippie and former magic mushroomer — this made perfect sense. At the time, I was even sleeping with the Bible under my pillow expecting to absorb it into my mind! However, I discovered that all that did was give me a stiff neck. So, after that failed, I just started reading it.

5. The preacher's name was John Bunyan. *Pilgrim's Progress* has become second only to the Bible in numbers of English language books printed in the last 300 years. I guess that their attempt to shut him up backfired on them.

men," the only explanation that they could find for their boldness was that they "... had been with Jesus" (Acts 4:13).

By saying this about the disciples, the religious leaders had unknowingly paid them a great compliment. These Ugly Preachers had been accused of hanging out with Jesus! The religious leaders could find no other explanation for how these common fishermen, who had never been to rabbinical school, could know and teach the Scriptures in such a personal and powerful way. Their only conclusion was that this Jesus — who the religious leaders could not seem to keep in the grave — had infected the disciples.

One of these disciples, John, later testified about living with the "Word of Life." He wrote, "That which was from the beginning, which we have *heard* [with the sound still ringing in their ears], which we have *seen* with our eyes [with the image still burning in them], which we have *looked* at [intently] and our hands have *touched* [and still feel the warmth of his skin] — this we proclaim to you concerning the *Word of Life*" (1 John 1:1, emphasis added).[6] Yes, they had "been with Jesus" and that is the primary preparation and training that enables anyone to share the message of this "Word of Life." God's preachers do not preach the lifeless words of human intellect, but they share the overflow of the life that they have experienced with Jesus — they are not head-talkers, but heart-talkers. Reggie McNeal, in his wonderful book for leaders, discussed this need for "heart-of-God-knower's" writing, "The ultimate responsibility of the spiritual leader is to share the heart of God with the people of God. This cannot happen if the leader does not know the heart

---

6. John uses the perfect tense (for the words heard, seen, touched) in explaining his experience with Jesus. This tense describes an action or event that happened in the past, and the results are still being experienced in the present. It is like someone ringing a bell once in the past and the sound still ringing in their ears today.

of God. This kind of intimacy comes from an intentional and frequent cultivation of a personal relationship that draws from every life experience."[7]

This is what prepared and qualified Jesus to come to earth and make it "known" (John 1:18) to us who God the Father is. The word that John used means to "draw out and make clear the meaning of something." Theologians use the term *exegesis* when they refer to studying the Scriptures and bringing out their meaning with a clear explanation. This is what Jesus did for us — he exegeted the Father for us. John told us that Jesus was able to so clearly and accurately "exegete" the Father to us because he "... is in the bosom of the Father" (John 1:18 KJV). Throughout eternity the Word has been "with God" (John 1:1), in the Father's bosom. John uses the same word, "bosom," to refer to himself laying his head on Jesus' chest at the Last Supper (John 13:23). The way to know the Father is to crawl up on to Jesus' lap, put your head on his chest, listen to his heart beat, and call him "Daddy."

This is how Peter and John were able to exegete the Scriptures-they laid their heads on the chest of the Living Word, Jesus, and listened to the father's heart, beating like a drum, saying, "I love you," (sounding much like a well known Rod Stewart song).[8] This is the song that we will hear as we press our face into his chest and listen for his heart. After hearing the rhythm of his heart, we are qualified to go and sing his love song to a hurting world; that is Ugly Preaching!

In Acts 3, Peter and John healed a crippled man and then

---

7. Reggie McNeal, *A Work of Heart: Understanding How God Shapes Spiritual Leaders* (San Francisco, CA: Jossey-Bass, 2000), 34.

8. Rod Stewart, *Rhythm of My Heart*, Vagabond Heart (Warner Bros., 1991).

boldly proclaimed that it was Jesus, who had been crucified not long ago, who had performed the healing. Jesus was back in business after the resurrection, except now all he had to work through were flawed and uneducated Ugly Preachers who heard the rhythm of his heart and allowed him to sing his love song to the world through them. Can you hear the music?

The Apostle Paul is considered one of the smartest men who ever lived, yet he described his preaching this way: "When I came to you brothers, [and sisters], I did not come with eloquence or superior wisdom as I proclaimed to you the testimony about God … I came to you in weakness and fear, and with much trembling. My message and my preaching were not with wise and persuasive words, but with a demonstration of the Spirit's power, *so that* your faith might not rest on men's wisdom but on God's power" (1 Cor 2:1-5, emphasis added). That is Ugly Preaching!

This isn't an excuse for shallow, sloppy, half-hearted, and unprepared preaching that lacks any content. If it's empty of meaning, it is just noise — no matter how loud you turn it up; volume, sweat, and even technology are not substitutes for the heart of God. The Ugly Preaching that Paul spoke of is preaching that aims at the heart more than the head. It's not preaching that fills in the blanks on a sermon sheet just to make points — it is preaching that awakens the dead! "… Prophesy to these bones and say to them … come to life" (Ezek 37:4-5). It is life transforming — world-changing words from God's heart spoken in the power of the Spirit through humble messengers. Bishop Tom Wright wrote of this type of preaching:

> …I believe, in other words, that Paul's gospel, and the doctrine of justification which follows closely and inescapably from it, have the power to do for the world and the church of today what they did in Paul's own day.
>
> Of course, that will demand persons willing to take the

risk of copying Paul: of being wise fools, strong weaklings, failures in human terms. If Christians are to preach the gospel, they cannot expect to be exempt from living the gospel. [9]

D. L. Moody, a great evangelist who lived over a hundred years ago, told the story of preaching at a church and afterwards receiving a letter from a religious expert that criticized his sermon, finding too many grammatical mistakes. He had counted thirty-nine errors and asked, "How can a man call himself a preacher and so butcher the King's English?" Moody's reply was simple and to the point — just like his preaching, it aimed at the heart not the head, "Sir, as I recall there were over twenty people who gave their lives to Christ that night, in spite of my many grammatical errors. I wonder how many people last week did you bring to Jesus with your perfect grammar?" I would have loved to have seen the expression on the man's face as he struck a sprinkler and went down in all of his grammatical pride.

Billy Graham tells the story of the donkey that Jesus rode into Jerusalem; as all of the people were cheering for him, the donkey mistakenly thought that they were cheering for him. He thought that they were laying palm branches in his path, and even placing their own coats on the ground, just to keep his precious hooves from touching the dirty soil. They were shouting some unknown word of praise to him, but that did not matter because he was the focus of all their attention:

"Hosanna to the son of David!"

"Blessed is he who comes in the name of the Lord!"
(Matt 21:9)

Applause and praise can be so intoxicating; we become drunk on the lie that it's all about us. Of course, we see clearly that the

9. N. T. Wright, *What Saint Paul Really Said: Was Paul of Tarsus the Real Founder of Christianity?* (Grand Rapids, MI: Eerdmans, 1997), 165.

crowd wasn't cheering for that ugly donkey, but for the glorious King of kings who rode on his back. But when it is us that he rides on, and people are shouting praise, it is so easy to start drinking it in. We can begin to deceive ourselves, just as the donkey did. We can all, especially Christian leaders, forget who is riding on our backs and develop Donkey Syndrome – thinking, "It is all about me."[10]

I take speaking God's word very seriously, and have been doing it for over thirty-five years — but I am no big deal. I'm not the focus, or as Lance Armstrong points out in his autobiography, "It is not about the bike, it is the rider that makes the difference."[11]

Ugly Preaching is not stupid, shallow, or superficial. It is a raw, down-to-earth, simple, practical, passionate, and unpolished presentation of the life-giving truths of God's word. Ugly Preaching is the beauty of the treasure of God, the glory of Christ, shining out through the broken places of our lives, as light escaping from cracks in clay jars (2 Cor 4:6-7).

In one of my favorite stories in the Old Testament, God chastised a prophet who thought he was a big deal. God didn't do this in any normal way though — he spoke words of rebuke to him from the mouth of the donkey he was riding (Num 22)! These were life-saving words to the prophet, who was headed for serious trouble. When God decided to warn him, he did not do it from the lips of another "man of God," but from the lips of an "ass of God."

I decided years ago to be an "ass of God." He can ride me when he wants, where he chooses, and how he pleases. My

---

10. At this point, beware of God's spiritual colonics. He knows just how to clean us out when we are blocked up with spiritual pride. Remember the White Castle burgers!

11. The difference in this analogy is that Lance, as the rider, is the important one; yet we are the bikes and Jesus is the rider, and it is not about us.

responsibility is to be ready so that I can go when he says "Giddy-up." No matter how or where he chooses to use us, it is never about the donkey.

* * *

Several years ago, someone finally saw the light and invited me to be the main speaker at a large Christian retreat with hundreds of people in attendance and many more watching on a closed-circuit television. It was my big opportunity! The doors had finally opened! This was the largest audience that I had ever spoken in front of; it may not have been Monday Night Football, but I was about to get caught picking my nose. At the time, I was pastoring a church with less than one hundred people, which, for whatever broken reason, made me feel like an insignificant failure.

I was preaching about not making big deals out of little things — something religious people are notorious for. Religious people have a tendency to fight the wrong battles, major on the minors, and always feel that the other person's breath smells worse than theirs. So in my unscripted, "anointed" style of preaching, I made the point that more people would be offended if I said the word "shit" than if I gossiped or spoke judgmentally, pridefully, or dishonestly.

I was right. It didn't matter what the rest of my points were that night, the audience was choking to death on that one little four-letter word. I had made my point way more clearly than I had expected! Now, I'm not blaming the word choice on the Holy Spirit and "the anointing," it could have just been Ugly Jamie. But give me unorganized, passionate, and authentic preaching with bad grammar, four letter words, and ADD over the polished words of a cold heart any day. Those cold hearts commit one of the greatest sins any preacher can be guilty of — being boring!

How can anyone who has tasted the "liquid love"[12] of God — anyone who has had their blind eyes opened by Jesus' amazing grace and experienced the life-changing power of the Holy Spirit — talk about God as though it were a eulogy? It may be eloquent, but it's lifeless. It may be complex and deep, but it is irrelevant. Pretty preachers need to heed the words of one of my heroes, C. H. Spurgeon, who was a contemporary and friend of D. L. Moody:

> Let the preacher always confess before he preaches that he relies upon the Holy Spirit. Let him burn his manuscript and depend upon the Holy Spirit. If the Holy Spirit does not come to help him, let him be still and let the people go home and pray that the Spirit will help him next Sunday.[13]

I know there are great communicators of God's word who are scripted and are far better preachers than I am; but I believe that the coming generation needs an ugly model that lowers the bar of what it takes for God to use us. I want young people to listen to my Ugly Preaching and think, "I can do that; anyone can do that." And they can, as long as they are willing to look like the ass of God to the religious world. Sick, broken, hurting, lost people are not seeking pretty doctors to heal their sick souls. They just want authentic, effective healers. Just as one beggar saying to another, "Here is some bread," imagine one sinner saying to another, "Here is where I found mercy." That is Ugly Preaching!

I'm a terrible dancer. I have no rhythm and way too much

---

12. Charles G. Finney, *The Autobiography of Charles G. Finney* (Grand Rapids MI: Bethany House Publishers, 1977).

13. John Stott, *Between Two Worlds: The Challenge of Preaching Today* (Grand Rapids, MI: Eerdmans, 1994), 334. John Stott writes that Spurgeon, as he climbed the steps to his pulpit, would whisper the words, "I believe in the Holy Ghost," then he would take another step and repeat the confession of faith, "I believe in the Holy Ghost." This is from a message that Spurgeon preached on June 20, 1858 entitled "The Outpouring of the Holy Spirit."

self-consciousness. I see how stupid other people look, and I get embarrassed for them. Yet I see preaching (or any work for God) as dancing before the Father; just as King David danced in complete surrender and humility before the ark — which represented the presence of God (2 Sam 6:14). David laid aside his royal garments and danced with all his might and passion before the God of the universe. He danced half-naked before God, exposing all of his scars, weaknesses, blemishes, and his ugly humanity. David knew the freedom of having his sins covered by the grace of God. David's dancing looked ugly in the eyes of many, especially his self-righteous wife who despised watching him humiliate himself in front of his subjects (2 Sam 6:16). Many years ago, Alexander Whyte described those cold-hearted, self-righteous, religious people: "Those who are deaf always despise those who dance." But those who hear the music, the rhythm of his heart beating like a drum, throw off all of their religious clothes and dance unhindered before God, as you share his word of life — this is Ugly Preaching.

Let me leave you with a few ingredients for the recipe for Ugly Preaching:

- Ugly Preaching is only an overflow of our relationship with God. We must know God and his heart before we can speak for him. This requires that we spend time alone with him, laying our heads on his chest, and listening to his heart.
- Ugly Preaching is always preaching the word. Not about it, not points and principles but saying, "this is what the Lord says." Our authority is never in us, but in the message of Jesus we preach.
- Ugly Preaching is a demonstration of the Spirit's power, not a display of our wisdom. It is not about volume or style; it is about dependency on his Spirit. We prepare as though God is not going to help us, and we preach as though we did not prepare!

- Ugly Preaching is a dance before the Father. He is the audience — not the people who are listening. We preach to please only him, and refuse to fall into the trap of the fear of man, or the bondage of trying to be a people pleaser.
- Ugly Preaching must be authentic, real, raw humanity. Pull your pants down and expose your scars, weaknesses, and failures. Ministry in the kingdom flows out of the grace we have discovered through our weaknesses — we are what Henri Nouwen calls "wounded healers."[14]
- Ugly Preaching laughs at yourself. Humor is humility with a smile. We take God seriously, but we are no big deal, and we are always our best material for sermon illustrations. We tell stupid stories that highlight our weaknesses and the need for his grace. Laughter is medicine and this broken world needs a huge dose! As John Ortberg says, "People are hungry for joy-bringers."[15]
- Ugly Preaching makes the call to Christ. We preach with the weight of eternity in the balance; people must be called on to decide whom they will serve.[16] As I have often heard Bill Hybels say, "Lost people matter most to God."[17] We get the great honor to call lost people home, into the welcoming arms of the Father.
- Ugly Preaching is what the man healed of blindness did to the religious experts who drilled him for theological answers

14. Henri J. M. Nouwen, *The Wounded Healer: Ministry in Contemporary Society* (New York, NY: Image Books, 1972).

15. John Ortberg, *Everybody's Normal Till You Get To Know Them* (Grand Rapids, MI: Zondervan, 2003).

16. Garrison Keillor once said, "The preaching of our day is friendly but of no use… too much preaching sounds as if nothing is at stake."

17. Bill Hybles, *Just Walk Across the Room*, (Grand Rapids, MI: Zondervan Publishing Company, 2006). Bill unpacks this heart for the lost in his great book.

about Jesus. His defense to them was not based on knowledge or information, but on personal experience. "... Whether he is a sinner or not, I don't know. One thing I do know. I was blind but now I see" (John 9:25)! A person with an experience of God's grace is never at the mercy of someone with an intellectual argument. Anyone who has experienced the life-changing love of Jesus can be an Ugly Preacher — just tell your story.

- Ugly Preaching is being willing to be his donkey. Let King Jesus ride you wherever he chooses, to speak to whomever he wishes. Remember that it is never about the donkey, but the One who rides it. Just be the "ass of God," for his glory!

....

The meat is in the street.

— John Wimber

Chapter 13. Ugly Evangelism

My 911 Call

I passionately proclaimed God's Word — feeling much like Billy Graham — as I held up my Bible to reinforce my authority as "the man of God," the evangelist. The difference was that my crusade was not in a football stadium filled with thousands of expectant people. I was preaching in a City Rescue Mission with about twenty hardcore street-people in attendance.

Since the day I surrendered my heart to Jesus and made the Ugly Exchange, I have carried a burden to share his love and good news with everyone. My early models of preachers were men who were serious, authoritative, and passionately against evil. There's nothing wrong with this, except that the message of Jesus was often preached with little mercy. They were angry with sinners whom they called "the lost" — as though they were coughing up something nasty. So I took up this model of preaching hard against all of the evils of our culture with a deep sense of moral superiority, as I stood for righteousness. The list of what I was against was much longer than the list of what I was for.[1]

---

1. Jack Taylor, a wise man of God, once gave me this warning: "If you find your purpose in life through being opposed to something, when what you are opposed to no longer exists, you will no longer have any purpose to live for." He went on to add that we should spend most of our time being *for* whatever it is that Jesus died for and what we will be doing for all eternity. Wise words that I wish I had heard earlier in my ministry. Jack was the one who first planted the

Truth can be so destructive without love. It's like having a dentist perform a root canal without any Novocain. Not only do you hear the awful sound of the drill and smell the horrible stench of a burning tooth, but the pain will almost kill you. Mercy is like spiritual Novocain; it brings comfort to the wounds that truth must cause to heal a sinful heart. Some spiritual leaders have opted for a message of mercy-without-truth approach to spiritual healing for a "pain free" approach to salvation. These people discover that the spiritual disease is still present in the heart. It is like taking laughing gas and not receiving the root canal; you experience a great high, but when it wears off the tooth is still rotten!

I was preaching *at* these addicted, evil sinners — giving them hardcore truth without mercy.[2] I was winding up for my big ending, which featured a call to accept Jesus, when I noticed that one of the roughest looking old men had fallen asleep again. He had been in and out of consciousness during my message, so every time I saw his head began to bob in slumber, I would shout my next words just to startle him awake. I wanted the end of this message to be heard by all, so I shouted again to wake him. Then, this crusty old man leaned, ever so slightly, to one side, grimaced

---

seed of The Power of Ugly in my heart through his message, "The Strength of Weakness, and the Weakness of Strength."

2. I have never spent a single night in my life as a homeless person. I had never once stopped to feel what they must have been going through. All I wanted at this time was a few more notches' on my Bible from conversions. These homeless men were required to listen to the sermon before they could receive the hot meal. (Can you say "bait and switch?") I did not care, however, because I had a captive audience that night to listen to the "next" Billy Graham as he mightily proclaimed the message of Jesus. I had come to set the captives free, raise the dead, and save the sinners; not because I cared anything about them as real human beings, but because they were *the lost*. I did not take time to hear any of their stories or to feel some of their hopelessness and pain. I was only there to "save them," so that I could go back to seminary and brag about the results.

for a moment, and with a look of deep relief fell right back into his slumber. There was no noise to give anyone an advance warning of the coming toxic fumes. It was silent but deadly! Those sitting right next to him were "blessed" first with the foul stench, and they jumped up screaming, "Oh my God, who died?" They ran out of that Rescue Mission, the hope of a hot meal gladly sacrificed so that they could escape the Stephen King Fart that came out with seven heads on it.

At first, I was unsure of what was happening. I thought that it was some kind of demonic attack that was robbing these lost souls from hearing my life-changing sermon (even though they had heard it a thousand times before). I continued preaching to a rapidly diminishing congregation until it was just the old man and me. It was then that the toxic smell hit me, and I quickly joined those fleeing from the evil odor. The old man, who had endured until the end of my message, was sleeping peacefully, desperately in need of some new underwear.[3]

I left the Rescue Mission discouraged; feeling like the devil had won by creating that foul smell from hell and disrupting my anointed preaching. As believers, it is too easy and convenient to see everything that bothers us as the devil. We give him way too much credit. Don't get me wrong — I know we are in a spiritual war that is more serious than any war that has ever been fought. However, our focus must always be on the greatness of our God and what he is doing, not on our enemy.

This deadly gas may have been the devil's work, or just the aged intestines of an old alcoholic,[4] but I believe that it, ultimately, was

---

3. Here is some insight for those who like secret knowledge: What is the secret as to why God made farts smell? So that deaf people would not miss the blessing!

4. Gritsch, *The Wit of Martin Luther*, 114. "Out of a desperate ass never comes a cheerful fart."

the work of God! You see, no matter whom or what has attacked us, our heavenly Father is greater and able to bring good out of the bad. I believe God had a hard lesson to teach one of his sons. This might stretch or offend some of you, but I think God was laughing at the whole scene. He was not laughing at the pain of these broken men, but at the arrogance of this young preacher. I've come to believe that the fart was a message from God, carrying with it his opinion of my preaching. My message was filled with Bible verses, but it was devoid of the greatest ingredient in the good news of Jesus: *love.*

Shouting at sick people to tell them that they are sick is spiritual insanity. They know better than anyone how desperate they are. Those men needed a hug. They needed someone to weep with them. They needed hope that God had not given up on them like everyone else had. They needed the father of the lost son that Jesus speaks about in Luke 15. They needed to feel the Father run to them and embrace them in his mercy, kissing them in all their ugliness. "... Mercy triumphs over judgment" (Jas 2:13)!

This fart began my long journey into discovering the heart of God, learning what is most precious to him on this planet — lost people. The religious leaders of Jesus' day could not understand why he loved hanging out around sinners and why sinners loved being with him. How would you like it if the type of people that loved to hang around you were the same as those who hung out with Jesus? Would you go to a church that was made up of all the types of people that Jesus attracted? Maybe a better way to ask the question is: Why aren't these people hanging out with us? Why aren't they being attracted to our churches? Have we become so pretty that the broken and outcasts of our society do not feel welcome among us? These questions keep me up at night. I am haunted by the question: "If Jesus lived in our city, would he attend the church that I pastor?" Jesus ate and laughed with these people. He listened to their stories, felt their pain, and endured their nasty farts. He gave them hope for a new life.

*   *   *

Where were you on September 11, 2001? I was doing what I do every Tuesday morning. I meet with a group of faithful men to pray for the needs of our church. Just as we had finished praying, we received the news that a plane had flown into the World Trade Center. Like everyone else, we stopped what we were doing and found a TV, only to watch in horror as the second plane collided with the other tower.

In the days that followed, I found myself, like many others, before the Lord asking what all of this meant. I was looking for some profound insights to announce to my church, to give some prophetic clarity to these horrible events. The TV preachers sure seemed to know what God was up to. They loudly proclaimed that this was God's judgment, saying that God had allowed these acts of terrorism because of a few particular sins in America. How dangerous and arrogant it is to presume to speak for God! Yet, as God's ambassadors, this is what we are called to do (2 Cor 5:20). We must first hear his heart before we share his message. Even if we have the message from God right, it's just as important to have the heart of how he wants us to share it.

This was a time our nation needed comfort and hope, not the "wrath of God." We needed to weep with those who wept, and grieve with those who grieved. Before we look out of the window and proclaim, "Thus saith the Lord," we must first look into the mirror and ask, "Lord, what do you want to say to me?" We must, with great humility, (admitting our own brokenness and the often clogged filters we hear through) cautiously say, "This is what I think the Lord is saying." We should always lay our hearts before the Lord, asking him, "Search me, God, and know my heart;... " (Ps 139:23). Jesus warned us by saying that you must always "... first take the plank out of your own eye, and then you will see clearly to remove the speck from your brother's eye" (Matt 7:5).[5]

I knew that this was a serious time for our country and the church. I realized that God was not asking me to explain the *why* of the evil to the whole world, but I did have a responsibility to lead a local church that needed direction from the Lord (1 Pet 4:17). So I laid out my heart before the Father and asked, "What does 9-11 mean to me?" The next words that I heard in my heart startled me. I heard the Lord say, "Jamie, you don't care about the world! You only care about your little kingdom and the church that you lead in Cape Coral." Even though I initially felt like arguing with God and giving him all my excuses, I didn't, because I've learned over the years that trying to argue with God is futile. He is never wrong, and he's a terrible negotiator.[6]

God had pierced me to the core of my heart. "I don't love the world!" He knows that I am much like Jonah who cared more for his selfish desires than he did for his enemies that were far from God. If he would leave me to myself, I would run and hide in

---

5. One day my wife started screaming in pain as though I was beating her. We were in an argument, but it was no big deal, except that she kept rolling back and forth as if I was striking her. She informed me it was the plank sticking out of my eye that was assaulting her. I, of course, humbly repented to her saying, "Thank you for pointing out that wonderful truth to me." Not!

6. It is like trying to convince your wife that she is wrong when she tells you, "I just don't feel like you love me." All of my great arguments, all of my lists of sacrificial duties, all of my debating is not the answer. She just needs to hear — with a sincere heart reaching out to hold her — "I'm sorry, honey. How can I better show you my love?"

our "Little Bear Cabin" in the mountains of Northeast Georgia. I would sit there on my porch with a shotgun firing it into the air if a stranger dared step foot onto my property, shouting, "Get the hell off my land!" I am so grateful that God loves me too much to leave me the way he found me, just as the lost son's father loved his son in all his ugliness, kissing away his shame. He did not leave him in the state that he had come home in; he loved him too much. The Father demanded, "... Quick! Bring the best robe and put it on him. Put a ring on his finger and sandals on his feet" (Luke 15:22).[7]

God is not just on a mission to pull lost people out of their darkness and pain; there is more to salvation than forgiveness. There is restoration of things that have been robbed from us. God's salvation is a process of restoring all of Creation to himself, transforming it for "... the glorious freedom of the children of God" (Rom 8:21).

God would not let Jonah have his own selfish, isolated, independent way. When he said go to the great city of Nineveh (now Iraq), he was calling Jonah to step out of all his elitist religious pride in being part of the chosen race and go to the lost — those whom he hated, the enemies of God. Jonah, like most of us, had to learn the hard way — in the belly of some whale — that nothing matters more to God. Not our comfort, happiness, prosperity, success, health — nothing matters more than the lost. They are the ones that God sent his Son "... to seek and to save" (Luke 19:10).

"Jamie, you don't care about the world!" I began to cry as he exposed to me the coldness of my heart. How could a pastor become so indifferent to the cries of the lost world? This kind of

---

7. Nothing in the universe is quicker than the warp speed of God's mercy. When God hears the words, "help me," nothing can stop the power of his rescuing love.

indifference is something that you can easily become infected with if you hang around the church very much. It is the corruption of our spiritual lives, as they have been turned inward, going deeper in the word and prayer, but forgetting the lost.

It is a religious disease where we become like the "us four and no more" lepers in the Old Testament (2 Kgs 7). These dudes were starving to death as the people of God had been under siege for months and the city had run out of food. It was so desperate that people inside the walls of the city had resorted to eating children! These four lepers were not even allowed to live within the protection of the city walls because of their disease, so they lived outside, near the gates, so that they could beg as people came and went. From time to time, a kind soul would throw some slop over the wall to feed them like dogs, but in the famine, even the slop had run out. In complete desperation, these guys decided to stop waiting to die and instead to go and turn themselves in at the enemy's camp, begging for mercy. They decided that they would certainly die if they stayed put, so at least they might have a chance if the enemy decided not to kill them. Either that hope would come true or they would die at the hand of their enemies, but just sitting there was not an option.

As they approached the camp, they discovered that not only were all the enemy soldiers gone, but they had left behind all of their possessions. Unknown to them, the Lord had sent angels to make the enemy army think that an even greater army was attacking them, so they fled in fear, leaving everything. These lepers had the buffet of their lives, gorging themselves on the enemy's left-behind food and hiding the treasures they found. Eventually they lay down, so full that they could not move. But then the voice of conscience began to speak to one of them. "... We're not doing right. This is a day of *good news* and we are keeping it to ourselves" (2 Kgs 7:9, emphasis added). They were shaken out of the selfish indulgence of their "us four and no more" mentality through the foul odor of their selfishness.

They went back to the walled city to announce that they had discovered the great victory of God over all their enemies. Of course, the people doubted these Ugly Evangelists as they announced the good news that the siege was over. So they began to throw food that they had gathered from the enemy's tents over the wall as proof of what they said. These four show a beautiful picture to us of what it requires to be an Evangelist — a messenger of good news.

First, you experience the good news personally — you "taste and see that the Lord is good" (Ps 34:8). Then you have to overcome the religious disease of "us four and no more." One author calls this disease "Koininitis,"[8] from the Greek word used for Christian community in Acts 2. Koininitis is what happens when we turn the church into a fortress as we hide in fear from the very world we are called to reach. We go deeper and deeper in our knowledge of the Bible as we pray for the rapture to come and snatch us out of this world before it goes to hell. This isolationist mentality is graphically illustrated in the movie *The Village*, where people are literally held captive in their supposedly utopian society by fear of venturing outside to the evil world around them. In the same way, many in the church today remain stuck in their Christian ghetto with an us-against-them mentality, withdrawing, hoarding the only hope from those living outside their fortress.

Christian community, or fellowship, is wonderful, and is a part of belonging to Jesus. However, it is not meant to be the Love Boat, where we all feast on our blessings and keep asking for more

---

8. C. Peter Wagner, *How to Have a Healing Ministry without Making Your Church Sick* (Ventura, CA: Gospel Light, 1988).

and more. We, as Abraham, have been blessed to be a blessing (Gen 12:2). We must hear the voice of God telling us "What you are doing is not good. You cannot hoard all of this." This is the message the Father was telling me as I prepared my sermon. Receiving the cure — the good news of the grace of God healing our sick hearts — obligates us to share the cure with others (Rom 1:14).

I began to repent before the Lord, asking him to forgive me for my selfish, cold, unloving heart. I had never prayed for the children in Iraq. I was actually thrilled when we began to bomb those "terrorist bastards." God wept over the destruction and death in Iraq while many of the Christians in America rejoiced. Sadly, we are often better Americans than we are Christians. What is sadder still is that I had never shed a tear or offered up a prayer for the hundreds of thousands of people killed in the genocide in Rwanda. I didn't even know where that was. I was like much of the church in Germany — asleep or looking the other way as Hitler killed millions of Jews.[9] As long as it doesn't affect our little selfish kingdoms, we just change the channel and watch reruns of *Everybody Loves Raymond*.

After asking for mercy, I asked God to change my heart and to tell me what he wanted me to *do*. It is not enough to have your sins forgiven — God wants to change us through his grace to make us more like Jesus! I also repented before our church for not leading them to love the things that Jesus loves — the lost, especially our lost enemies. We all repented of our us-four-and-no-more hearts and asked the Lord to use us as he used those Ugly [Leper] Evangelists who became the messengers of good news.

---

9. Yancey, *What's So Amazing About Grace?*, 178. "When someone asked theologian Karl Barth what he would say to Adolf Hitler, he replied, 'Jesus Christ died for your sins.'"

Our church, just like their pastor, is in the process of being cured of "Koininitis." We now realize that we have a sacred obligation to share the blessings that we have received from the Lord. As a part of that sacred obligation, our members now partner with World Vision to sponsor over one hundred children in the Democratic Republic of Congo, we have teams going to Cuba regularly, to partner with the church there, and we have opened up a Hope Center in our church to feed hot meals to those in need four days a week during our city's worst economic crisis in its history. We have hundreds of people coming through the Hope Center each week receiving love, prayer, and a hot meal; and that is the message. Our people, many of whom are unemployed themselves, serve these hurting people. They hug them, listen to their stories, pray for them, and show them the love of Jesus. That is the "sermon" they have to listen to before we feed them.

Evangelism is about sharing the good news of our heavenly Father who is like the dad in Luke 15 who cared more about the lost son than anything else. In all of our weekend celebration services, we end with a call to act on the good news, confessing Jesus as Lord. When people decide to step across the line of faith into a new beginning, we ring a huge bell outside joining in the celebration of the Father who sings with a joy that fills all of creation over just one lost sheep who has come home to him.

I can't speak for all of the church; but for me and our Ugly Church, September 11th was a wake-up call to start caring. It doesn't matter how broken we are when we experience the grace of God in our lives. We can become Ugly Evangelists just as the four lepers did. We just tell our stories of grace and throw a spiritual chicken leg over their walls of fear so that they can "taste and see that the Lord is good" (Ps 34:8 and 1 Pet 2:3).

Dear Father, as much as we think we would like to be left alone to do our own things — to just be happy in our own little selfish world — help us, shake us, awaken us, drag us out of our selfish isolation. Move us beyond our Christian ghettos and into this hurting world that desperately needs the hope that we have found in you. Forgive us for hoarding this hope. Take us as the little child's five loaves and two fishes — bless us, break us, and then multiply us to feed the hungry world. Amen.

Even if it takes some awful, foul odor to wake us up, let it pass!

Marriage is the operation by which
a woman's vanity and a man's egotism
are extracted without anesthetic.
— Helen Rowland

Chapter 14. Ugly Marriage

Maybe You Are the Antichrist

Let me say with all honesty, I have a beautiful bride that is a gift from God.[1] The Lord, in his mercy, blinded her from seeing my ugliness long enough so that I could get her to marry me. Sadly, for both of us, those blinders did not last long! We only courted for three months before we married — I knew the time would come when she would see the light. Or should I say darkness?

There is no one you will ever marry that is not a sinner — we all have a dark side. I heard about a middle-aged lady who thought that she had discovered her perfect soul mate — probably through some Internet dating service. She was engaged to this perfect match when, while on a business trip, he suddenly dropped dead from a heart attack. She was devastated with grief. She went back to his home to pick up some of her belongings and noticed the door to the basement that she had never gone into. With her Eve-like curiosity, she ventured down the stairs. When she turned on the light, she was horrified to discover nineteen fully dressed mannequins, and each mannequin was positioned in a lifelike pose! One was standing at a stove cooking, several were on couches

---

1. When we first kissed, I warned Kim with all humility, "Before you kiss me you should know that once you have tasted these lips, you will never want any others!" Let me just say that thirty plus years later, I am the only lips she has ever wanted. (I hope!)

talking, and one was still in bed sleeping. At the sight of this, she fled outside screaming, and called 911. Now I can only guess what she told the operator: "I need help; my fiancé has a basement full of mannequins, and you might find some bodies in the yard! Quick, send the cops!" At the discovery of the mannequins, her grief quickly turned into relief.

We all have a basement; yours may not be filled with mannequins, but you do have issues. If you do not allow Jesus to come in and clean out your basement, then the mannequins will come marching out to expose you at some point. I'm not sure when it happened, but not long into our marriage, the veil was lifted, and the mannequins came marching out. To Kim's horrible surprise, this holy man of God she married became the antichrist!

This makes me think of the scene in the all-time-best-ever western movie *Tombstone*. The doctor has just informed Doc Holiday (played brilliantly by Val Kilmer) that he was dying. The doctor advised him to rest, stop smoking and drinking, and to abstain from sexual relations. After the Doctor left, Doc's lover said to him, "Doc, ain't I good to you?" as she poured him a drink, lit up a cigarette, and slowly rubbed her hand up his thigh. Doc responded, "Yes, you are dear." He paused and then added, "But then again, you might be the antichrist."

Soon after Kim's horrible discovery of my mannequins, I received a call that I will never forget. My wife informed me, "I'm going to another church. I don't want you to be my pastor anymore." She also added that she agreed with the people who had left our church calling me a "false prophet!" We had been married for less than a year, and I was leading a Baptist church where I had already offended several of the members of this very small congregation, some of whom left the church declaring, "Jamie is a false prophet." Kim, before hanging up, said, "I am done trying to be spiritual for you. I'm listening to country music, smoking a cigarette, and I think you might be the antichrist!"

What do you do when your wife thinks that you are the antichrist? I usually try acting like one first, but for some reason that never worked very well. For thirty years we have journeyed together, raising three beautiful daughters, and currently have nine grandbabies. In the first years of our marriage, I taught a sermon series on "God's Ten Commandments for a Happy Home." After a few years of marriage and being called the antichrist, I changed the series to "Seven Secrets for a Happy Home." A few more years went by, with many more painful moments, and the series became "A Few Suggestions for a Happy Home." Then, after a separation, which almost ended in a divorce, my new series was "To Hell and Back: How to Stay Married by the Grace of God."

God has never made two more complete opposites than Kim and me. Why do opposites attract? You would think that you would want to marry someone just like you. I mean, I like me, I understand me, and I get along well with me. I always seem to agree with myself! I love to make me happy. Rarely do we need to see others' perspectives, because ours is always right. I and me — now that is a match made in heaven … or maybe hell.

The only thing that Kim and I are alike in is that both of us love Jesus. But we express our love for Jesus in completely different ways. (My ways are more spiritual, of course, and yes, I agree with me on this point!)

After thirty years of Ugly Marriage, I have no commandments to give you, no secret knowledge, no seven principles, just a few suggestions and some stories of discovering God's grace in the midst of the mess of marriage. Kim said to me the other day, "I hope you don't die on me anytime soon. It's been too hard to train you to become the man you are; I would hate to have to break in a new one." Somewhere in there, I think there was a compliment.

Marriage is messy. In fact, it's downright ugly at times. We must move from our dream of what a marriage should be to embrace the reality of what God is making it by his grace. To paraphrase Bonhoeffer's warning quoted in *Ugly Church*, those who love their dream of marriage more than the reality of marriage itself, become destroyers of marriage, even though their intentions may be ever so sincere. As Kim and I have journeyed through the valley of the shadow of death of our marriage, we have realized the raw reality that for two sinful people trying to do life together, it is going to be very painful at times. C. S. Lewis once said it this way:

"To love at all is to be vulnerable. Love anything and your heart will certainly be wrung and possibly broken."

* * *

Most of us marry for all of the wrong reasons:

"She makes me so happy."

"He is everything I have ever dreamed of."[2]

"He understands me and loves to just sit and talk with me."

"He is so patient with me and cares about whatever is going on in my life."

"This girl is so hot; she could be a swimsuit model!"

Charles Swindoll, in one of his sermons, describes the process of moving from fantasy love to the real world like this:

> When you are newlyweds and your spouse gets a cold you rush them to the hospital with the greatest concern. After a few years she gets a cold and you recommend that she call the doctor, still very concerned. As the years pass, you hear her sneezing and coughing; you say, 'Honey after you finish doing the dishes you should take something and get some rest.' Years later as she coughs, sounding to you much like a dog barking; so loud you can't even hear the TV! So you say

2. But he is soon to become your greatest nightmare!

to her, "Hey, would you go into another room? Your coughing is driving me crazy!

So where is the hope of the wine getting sweeter as it ages? This hope starts when your dreams of a romance-novel-marriage and his fantasies of being married to "I Dream of Jeannie," who always looks sexy and pops out of her bottle to fulfill her master's every wish, dies. It's when you begin to see how selfish your motives are and how warped your understanding of marriage is. No one signs up for marriage to learn how selfish, impatient, harsh, and unloving he or she really is. And yet, there is nothing else in the world like marriage when it comes to holding a mirror up to you to expose how ugly you are. (Unless you add having kids, but that's the next chapter). Marriage opens the door to the basements of our lives, inviting the mannequins to come on out.

Before I got married, I really thought of myself as a committed Christ follower, not quite a saint, but on my way. I had quit drugs, drinking, smoking, cursing (most of the time), and sleeping with girls. I was learning much of the Bible and could quote from memory many verses. I was feeling very pure, holy, and humble. I had not realized that quitting a few outward sins was, according to Jesus, not all there was to being holy — as the Pharisees were informed by him when he rebuked them: "Woe to you, teachers of the law and Pharisees, you hypocrites! You clean the outside of the cup and dish, but inside they are full of greed and self-indulgence. Blind Pharisee! First clean the inside of the cup and dish, and then the outside also will be clean" (Matt 23:25-26).

As marriage begins to expose in us the things on the inside that need cleaning out, there is much pain and disillusionment. Until you reach this point of desperation — crying out "O God, I can't love this person" — you'll never learn his unconditional, sacrificial, love. His love requires carrying the cross. This *Cross Love* is a love of choice, not feelings. It is a love that is not based on the other person's performance. Cross Love continues to give when the other person least deserves it. Cross Love forgives before the guilty partner ever says, "I'm sorry." Cross Love chooses what is best for the other at the expense of our own desires. Cross Love is the love Jesus gave for his bride, the church, as he died for her when she was at her worst. Jesus calls husbands to love as he loves — with Cross Love (Eph 5:25).

After nearly twenty years of marriage, my wife left me. In my pride and brokenness, I still thought the church couldn't make it without me, so I kept preaching while my wife was going through a breakdown. My "other woman" was my job — the church. Week after week I stood up there preaching even though it was hell for me. I had told the congregation that my wife had left me, and every Sunday I felt as though I was holding up a giant sign that said "hypocrite." Finally, I stepped down from pastoring — which was all I had ever known as an occupation. I had been a pastor my entire adult life. It was the toughest thing that I have ever done. I found an Ugly Altar and practiced dying to "being a pastor." I stepped into the unknown, with only his promise:

"Never will I leave you;
    never will I forsake you" (Heb 13:5).

I was broken, empty, and lonely. I had neglected my wife to minister to people who had already forgotten my name. I was just a picture in their photo album, performing their marriage ceremony or baptizing them. Looking at the pictures they said, "Remember that pastor? What was his name?"

"Yeah, the guy who told all those funny stories."

Then they just turned to the next page in their album. I was probably doing their wedding on my day off, neglecting the woman I had married.

I had to give up the church (not Jesus) to show my bride that she was more important than anything else in my life. Words were cheap, and she did not believe me until she saw me take up the cross and step down from the church. From the day that I stepped down, our marriage began to be restored.

At my first counseling appointment, I felt so much shame just being seen at a counselor's office. I had been the pastor and counselor to hundreds of people, giving out my "Secrets to a Successful Marriage." I just wanted to put a bag over my head — some kind of mask or fig leaf to cover me. The Lord, in my time of journaling, had given me a verse out of the Gospel of John that spoke about his Son taking up of the cross to die. "I tell you the truth, unless a kernel of wheat falls to the ground and dies, it remains only a single seed. *But* if it dies, it produces many seeds. The man who loves his life [the 'me and me' love affair] will lose it, while the man who hates his life [by giving it away for others] in this world will keep it for eternal life" (John 12:24-25, emphasis added).

As I walked into the counseling office with a bag over my head (well, I wanted one), I signed in, looking at all of the losers who really needed to be there. I was waiting for Jack Nicholson to stick his head in proclaiming, "What if this really is as good as it gets?" As I sat in the waiting room, I looked up in front of me and there, written on the wall, were the words from the Gospel of John that I had read that morning, "Except a grain of wheat falls to the ground and dies, it remains alone." It was God's invitation for me to realize what Dietrich Bonhoeffer says in his classic book, *The Cost of Discipleship*, "When Christ calls a man, he bids him come and die."[3]

Loving his bride, the church, cost Jesus everything. Loving

3. Dietrich Bonhoeffer, *The Cost of Discipleship* (New York, NY: Touchstone, 1995), 11.

others as he loves will cost us everything. It is the sacrificial love of the cross. I believe the main purpose for marriage is to make us like Jesus — not to make us happy. The way that God's kingdom works is that the more that I give, the more I receive. As Kim and I work at this thing called marriage — ugly as it is at times in all of our weaknesses — we are discovering the beauty of Jesus as we grow to be more like him. We are learning to receive one another as we are, and to trust God to make the necessary changes — even though he seems to take forever to make them. There is no magic, no silver bullet, no e-Harmony, and no secret. Just the power of his grace: "... My grace is sufficient for you, for my power is made perfect in weakness" (2 Cor 12:9). Celebrate the weakness in your marriage and how much you need his strength, and you will discover The Power of Ugly Marriage.

After thirty years, I can truly say, "Her breasts satisfy me always, I am always captivated by her love" (Prov 5:19 an interpretation).

Kim, I love you. Thank you for sharing this Ugly Journey with me. Thank you for being my beauty, as I am your beast.

....

Hold the people you love loosely....
Part of the thrill of guiding children
into adulthood is the release, but it's also
a parent's greatest act of surrender.
— Charles Swindoll

Chapter 15. Ugly Parenting

Just Give Me The Drugs

"Just breathe like we practiced, honey. Puff, puff, puff, and push."

"Shut up, you idiot!"

"But you need to breathe. Puff, puff..."

"I want the drugs!" The scream echoed down the hospital hallways, striking terror in the hearts of those poor expecting mothers who were waiting to go into labor. "Give me the drugs! I want the drugs! Just give me the drugs!" Kim demanded like a heroin addict in delirious withdrawals. The little old nurse tried to inform her, "Oh dear, it is too late for the drugs. The baby is coming!"

Where is the fine print that gives you the disclaimers for having babies, like the ones for prescription drugs in those stupid ads on TV? "May cause vomiting, loss of appetite, back pain, headaches, diarrhea, and brain damage. Contact your doctor before taking this medicine." No need to, you just talked me out of it! No one tells you the secret about parenting: kids will ruin your life. The birth pains are just a small taste of what is coming!

None of us sign up to be parents so we can lose sleep, give up our hobbies because we have no free time left, and then work two jobs just to feed and clothe the little blessings. You lose all of your friends who don't have kids, because they do not want to go see another animated movie. You end up at a place that you swore to God you would never visit — The Cabbage Patch Hospital — where you pay more for a doll than you did for your first car, God laughing the whole time!

I thought marriage had exposed all my selfishness and lack of love, but parenting was the knockout punch. God continued to laugh as he gave me back-to-back-to-back girls. These three daughters were the answers to all those dumb spiritual prayers I foolishly prayed as a new believer before someone warned me (too late of course) to stop. "Oh God, mold me, humble me, grind me to fine powder, make me like Jesus. Teach me patience, Oh Lord. Cause me to love others like you do." I never pray those prayers any more. I don't need to, because I can't withdraw the ones I have already prayed. God is mean!

I love my three girls, Kelly, Kristy and Kasey, with all my heart. They are three of the prettiest, sweetest, and most wonderful daughters a father could have ever dreamed of raising. Our biggest failure in parenting was the same one we committed in attempting to grow the church: we tried too hard in our own strength, not trusting enough in God's grace. We parented too much out of fear, trying to keep them in *The Village*. We did not want them to experience the same pain and heartbreak we had growing up.

We read everything in the Christian bookstore, and put every principle we found into practice with a militant commitment. We spanked, we threw out "evil" toys like Rainbow Brite, Glow Worms, and worst of all those Cabbage Patch dolls with their "demonic" names. All of this thanks to the great legalistic teaching of the "Basic Youth Conflict."[1] We turned off the Smurfs, fasted,

---

1. Maybe, Bill, the teacher, should have gotten married and had a few kids before he attempted to teach us all of the secret principles. I would like to put him over my knee and wear him out with a belt!

took them to church three days a week, ate green spaghetti, broke curses, and sang stupid songs very early in the morning, very loudly. "Arise and Shine and Give God the Glory, Glory!" We even broke the great evil lie to our children that Santa was a phony! We never allowed them to dress up and go trick-or-treating. No makeup, no dances, no dating, no kissing, no spending the night at anyone's house if they had not had a religious background check and could pass for a saint.

We meant well. We knew the darkness of what lay ahead of them in this evil world. But we trusted in rules as our protection. It may work with a compliant, passive, child; but not with our three strong-willed girls who were destined to grow into God's leaders for their generation. I knew the teenage years would be tough, but I had no idea how tough. As Kim said, "Giving birth was not nearly as painful as the spiritual labor pain you go through seeing your children turn away from all that you have taught them." You must labor in prayer and faith to see your children restored to Jesus. All of our daughters will tell you that they are alive today and walking with Jesus because of their mother's prayers. Mothers must travail both for physical birth and spiritual birth (Gal 4:19).

* * *

"What was that noise?" my wife asked in the middle of the night. We had become light sleepers, since our daughters had mastered the art of sneaking out of their windows at night to escape our prison. I heard it again, and I got up, thinking it was a burglar.[2] At this point in my parenting, I had become like the character Steve Martin portrayed in *Planes, Trains and Automobiles* when he was trying to rent a car. After enduring more than any human should

---

2. Thankfully, I did not have a gun that night or there would have been some dead bodies!

have to endure, he finally arrived back at the counter of the car rental company that had left him stranded in the freezing parking lot. With incessant background music playing and his inner voice repeating, "You're messing with the wrong guy," he finally snaps on the chubby lady behind the desk, dropping the f-bomb more times than the average rap song. That was me!

We lived in a two-story piling home. Our bedroom was on the top floor.[3] I ran (once again, all I was wearing were my tighty-whities) down the stairs and out the door to find a ladder leaning on the outside of our house under my middle daughter's bedroom window. She was fifteen years old at the time. Seeing a van parked on the street behind our house, I snapped. With a toxic combination of anger and fear, my eyes rolled back into my head as it spun around on my shoulders and green puke began spewing out of my mouth. I crashed through the bushes to get to the van. I can only imagine what that sight must have been to these teenagers — a nearly naked fat guy comes screaming and crashing through the bushes to the rescue of his poor, helpless daughter they were attempting to abduct (at least that was the way that I wanted to believe that it was happening).

I screamed (filled with the love of Jesus) at the large nineteen-

---

3. Thinking of that old piling home reminded me of an Ugly Sex story! We often had different people live with us as we were trying to help them. One time we had an extremely fragile and slightly O. C. D. girl living with us. As we went to bed one night, I decided to put in a load of clothes in the washer. The next morning she said, "Well, you had quite a night!" But I had no idea what she meant. A piling home is designed to give, so that it can survive strong winds. As the clothes washed, the machine shook the house while it went through the different cycles. This girl never thought about the laundry washing — she thought we were having sex! She thought the house shaking meant we were "getting busy" upstairs. She waited through the different cycles of the 45-minute wash thinking, "O my God, he is an animal. He is going to hurt Kim." Just when one cycle would end and she would begin to feel relief, the next one jolted her back into her panic. To this day, she does not believe that it was only the washing machine!

year-old boy, "What the hell are you doing?" I lunged at this young man, who was much bigger than myself, intending to tear his heart out. He could have killed me if it wasn't for the hand that grabbed me by the hair, yanked me back, and screamed "Jamie; don't hurt them!" (That would be my lovely bride, who, once again, threw on a housecoat first, and then quickly followed me outside. I had failed to notice that there were several other young guys with this punk, and I had no way to know that one of them had recently been released from prison for a violent crime.)

The look on those kids' faces was sheer terror, seeing a crazy, nearly naked guy whose wife was trying to stop him from killing them. They froze in fear, and then jumped into their van, taking off. Looking back on it, the only thing that saved me was The Power of Ugly — the insane look in my eyes, my tighty-whities, my fat body, and my wife's scream. The headlines in the Sanibel Newspaper could have read, "Fat, Naked Pastor Murders Innocent Boys." Throughout the years of my daughters' growing up, there were police calls, fights, drugs, and trips to jail. All of these had one common theme — boys. I learned to hate boys. I wanted to castrate all of them.

* * *

As the words to the song "I Hope You Dance" were playing,[4] I held my oldest child in my arms as we danced the father-daughter dance at her wedding. It was in this moment I remembered the simple words of wisdom a friend had given me as we were brokenhearted over the life she was living a few years earlier —

---

4. I will always treasure the dances I shared with my daughters at their weddings. Kasey and I danced to "Butterfly Kisses," Kristy and I to "I Loved Her First," and Kelly and I to "I Hope You Dance." These songs are so emotionally powerful that they should be outlawed.

stealing, drugs, raves, and so much more that I never want to know. He said, "Kelly is not going to have the story that you want to write for her. She is writing her own story, and she will have her own testimony about the grace of God." These wise words would prove so helpful on our journey with all three of our daughters. How painful it is to give up on our dreams and plans of the way we wish things would be, and surrender to the plans of God.

We dedicated all of our girls to the Lord after they were born, placing them back into God's hands. The problem was that it was so easy to take them back out of his hands and then just try harder to make them into what we wanted. Years later, as our girls were becoming teenagers, the Lord spoke to me as I was lying in bed: "I want you to give me your girls." I knew from the seriousness of his voice what this meant. He was asking me to put them on the altar as Abraham had done with his only son Isaac (Gen 22). God was asking for me to give him my children again, but now in a deeper way. One by one, Kelly, Kristy, and then Kasey; I gave them to God as I wept. I had no idea what the years ahead of us would hold, but God did, and he knew how essential it would be for us to remember that they all belonged to him.

During the teenage years, I called our home the "House of Emotions." I had a wife, three daughters, and a sissy dog. I took so many trips to the mini-market to get milk and tampons that the guy at the register began to look at me like he was wondering, "Is this guy eating these for breakfast?"

It is so painful to care deeply for another person. Some have opted to be alone to avoid the pain of marriage and parenting. The title to Dr. Dobson's great book says it all: *Parenting is not for Cowards*. There are not enough drugs to take away the pain of a child that has left the light to live in the darkness. Only God truly knows this pain, as so many of his children have chosen the wrong path in spite of all of his loving parenting. Knowing that God has rebellious kids gives me relief from the tremendous sense of failure I sometimes feel as a parent. It's not that we didn't do many stupid things as parents, but I know kids raised in the worst homes that you could imagine, with parents that deserved to be in jail, but, by the grace of God, they turned out to be great people in spite of their parents.

Jesus illustrated the Father's great love for children that go astray through the story of the father whose youngest son demanded his inheritance (Luke 15). He basically told his dad, "You're dead to me. All I want is your money." The father released the son with his money to go and write his own story. Letting go is so hard, and it requires a deep trust in the one to whom you have committed your children. As time passed, the boy wasted all his money and hit rock bottom. He lost all of his false lovers and friends, and then finally "... came to his senses,..." (Luke 15:17). He began heading home to the arms of the one he knew loved him. In just one verse of this story, we can discover more insight into the heart of our God as our Father than we could ever fully grasp: "... But while he was still a long way off, his father *saw* him and was *filled* with compassion for him; he *ran* to his son, threw his arms around him and *kissed* him" (Luke 15:20, emphasis added).

This is the God that Jesus came to reveal to us as our Father. This is our model of parenting. This should be the mission of every church, and every Christian, to be like this Father — a Father who never gives up hope on us, but watches every day, anticipating and longing for our return.

At the glimpse of his filthy, emaciated body, his heart burst — not with anger lashing out with the often-rehearsed lecture of "I told you so." His heart was filled with love on fire, the *Chesed*[5] of the Old

---

5. Peterson, *Leap Over a Wall*, 173. *Chesed* is the Hebrew word often translated as love or loving-kindness. It is a word so rich in meaning that no

Testament. It is filled with mercy that is new every morning (Lam 3:22). The Father's love — a love expecting nothing, only wanting to give.

In Jesus' story in Luke 15, he tells us that the Father "ran to his son" (Luke 15:20), something no dignified Hebrew man would ever do. Thankfully though, our Father is humble and not prideful or dignified. He runs to us! "Come near to God and he will come near [run] to you" (Jas 4:8).

This lost son was hugged to life by the Father's embrace, even before a bath to wash off the nasty pig slop — his smell of sin. He was pulled into the very bosom that Jesus left to come to earth to rescue us (John 1:18). Listening to the heart of the Father, beating like a drum, each heartbeat saying, "Welcome home, son. I've missed you!"

Then he kissed him over and over.[6] Why so many kisses from the Father? Because the son had so many doubts and shameful thoughts: "How could he love someone like me?" Kiss, and it was gone. "But I have wasted my life and shamed my Father!" Kiss, and it was washed away! Kisses cleanse so much deeper than lectures. Kisses soften hearts while yelling only hardens. Kisses reinforce discipline, not weaken it. Kisses bring life — they are the medicine that a prodigal needs.

* * *

---

one word in English can be used to translate it. Instead, we must revert to using adjectives to describe this wonderful word. Eugene Peterson describes *Chesed* as "love without regard to shifting circumstances, hormones, emotional states, and personal convenience" and, "this is love with covenant steel." *Chesed* is covenant love demonstrated beautifully in David's *chesed* for the only remaining relative of Saul. David showed undeserved love and kindness to the crippled Mephibosheth because he had made a promise to Jonathan, Mephibosheth's father. See 1 Samuel 20 and 2 Samuel 9.

6. The original Greek gives us this meaning.

I hope that these stories will give you hope that our heavenly Father is a faithful dad. We can trust him with those we love the most because he loves them more. Sorry there are no magic bullets or faith guarantees that if you do this and that you will have no problems with your kids.

I had a church member make an appointment to come see me for counsel for her teen. Later she called back to cancel the appointment, stating, "After seeing how your daughters are turning out [they were all still teens], I do not want to have you advise me on my teen." At the time, that was a very painful thing to hear, as it reinforced all the accusing voices that I was already hearing in my head. It is the devil's way to take a snapshot of our lives and use it to define us. The Lord, however, was in no way finished with our daughters; they were writing their own stories of grace.

Faith must look past the present to the hope of the future that God desires. Of course, there are many things we would do differently if we had it to do over again, that is why we are now called *grandparents*. Why do we not have a grandpa heart as a parent? Because it is all the failure, pain, and sorrow of being a parent that teaches us how to love with God's love; preparing us for grandparenting.[7]

As we learned in *Ugly Death,* because of the resurrection, we can have the hope that our "labor in the Lord is not in vain" (1 Cor 15:58). This includes all of the prayers, sacrifices, and tears. It includes the going-without so that they can have, the curfew arguments, the sleepless nights, and all that you have invested in

---

7. Henri J. M. Nouwen, *The Return of the Prodigal Son: A Story of Homecoming* (New York, NY: Image Books, 1994), 123. Actually, it is far more than preparing us to be grandparents. It is preparing us to become spiritual fathers and mothers to the many spiritual prodigals that are in the world. Henri Nouwen described this call to become spiritual fathers and mothers when he wrote, "I am destined to step into my father's place and offer to others the same compassion that he has offered me. The return to the father is ultimately the challenge to become the father."

raising your children. If we do it in his name, it will bear fruit for his glory. We may lose many battles, but with Jesus, we will not lose the war.

Let the encouraging words of the Apostle Paul help you to never give up: "Let us not become weary in doing good, for at the proper time we will reap a harvest *if* we do not give up" (Gal 6:9, emphasis added). The hardest times are living between the sowing (the doing good) and the reaping. We want to read the promise that "... whoever sows generously will also reap generously" (2 Cor 9:6), as if there is no waiting between sowing and reaping. But the way that it usually works is you sow; wait; cry out; feel like giving up; think, "This was all a waste;" and hear the lie, "Your faith and prayers are not making any difference." At the point of desperation, you pray "O, God. O, God. O, God. Help! Father, only you can bring them back. I give my children to you again and trust you with them." Finally, the miracle of resurrection begins to happen as you reap. This is laboring in the spiritual birth pains to see your children fulfill their God-given destinies (Gal 4:19). Never give up; our God is Faithful.

Kelly, Kristy, and Kasey: You are our treasures. We are so proud of you. We have seen you become beautiful women of God! But we have to be honest, we love those grandbabies more than you, and that is just the way it is!

The simple, profound secret to drawing
for every need, temporal or spiritual, upon
the "fathomless wealth of Christ."
— Hudson Taylor

Chapter 16. ugly secret

Banging Pots and Pans

Nothing tests a marriage more than camping. Attempting to set up a tent in a driving rain may seem romantic to a man, but to a woman, it's an absolute nightmare. We were camping deep in a national forest in North Carolina — where there are real live bears. Some veteran campers had told us that we needed to hang our cooler from a tree to keep it from the scavenging beasts, and they also shared their secret weapon, that if a bear did come in to the camp you should, "bang some pots and pans together, making a lot of noise — the bear will take off like a scared dog." So we confidently set up in the most remote corner of the campground, and after surviving a terrible storm the first night, we were ready for a good night's sleep.

We were awakened around 4 a.m. on the second night by a bear trying to get at our cooler. It seemed that hanging the cooler had just enraged the hungry animal. I had only tied the cooler about ten feet away from the tent, so we could hear everything the bear was doing. The first thing my wife asked me was if I had snuck any candy bars into the tent. I told her that I did have one, which created great fear because she knew that bears love Snickers. I also had another big problem — all the excitement had made me really need to pee.

Refusing to allow the bear to intimidate me, the John-Wayne-camper, I decided to put the "secret knowledge" to practice. With a flashlight under my arm and pots and pans in my hands, I unzipped the tent. I peered cautiously into the dark to see a 300-pound black bear tearing into our cooler. I shined the light on him with all the courage that I could muster and banged the pots as loud as I could, shouting at the bear. Let me just say the secret didn't work.

The bear turned, looked right at me, and gave me the finger (at least that's what it felt like). He roared back at me with no fear. He was not about to leave the treasures he had discovered in our cooler. With my secret weapon failing and desperately needing to relieve myself, I had no other choice. I stood at the door of the tent and peed right in front of the bear. I was trying to act manly, attempting to mark my turf. He must have taken this as a challenge, because he lunged towards me! This caused me to scream like a girl, and I instantly zipped up, unfinished, leaving a large wet spot, and retreated back into the tent. Kim and I huddled together in fear, praying to God as the man-eater, only separated from us by a thin piece of fabric, devoured all of our food.

By the time the sun came up, the bear had eaten his fill. He wandered a safe distance away, but not before gathering a crowd of other campers who had enjoyed watching him eat our provisions. When the coast was clear, we stepped out and began to survey the damage.

We had become the talk of the campground as "the couple that survived the bear attack!" Even the park ranger had come to congratulate us! He drove up in his truck and said to me, "Heard you had an encounter with a bear last night." I answered with a sense of camping pride, "Yes, we did." The ranger, in his southern drawl, responded, "I guess you weren't too scairt." I was enjoying this confirmation of my great courage when he continued, "I guess that's why you got that shirt on backwards." He spit out some tobacco juice and drove off laughing. It was at that moment I realized that I had put on a button-up shirt backwards like a hospital gown and, of course, I still had a large wet spot on my pants!

That secret proved to be a bunch of crap. Most secrets of the spiritual life work like the secret of the pots and pans; it might work for some people, but when it really counts, it never works for you. This is why I have referred to this book as Gnosticism in reverse. Gnosticism is the teaching that has secret knowledge for everything, and we all want those secret formulas so that we too can learn how to be a success in life. We want to find the secret to a good marriage or to parenting kids in such a way that they will never fall away from faith.

At this point, you have heard most of my stories, and probably realized that none of the "secret" ways have worked for me. Maybe if I was more disciplined, more spiritual, more positive, more holy, and certainly more faith filled, then these secrets would have done the trick. But God, in his mercy, lets *all* of our secrets fail us at one time or another so that we don't begin to worship the secrets instead of Jesus. The death of secrets can be a very unsettling experience, but it can lead to the real security of trusting in Jesus.

* * *

There is no greater quest in life than the quest for contentment. People are willing to spend all their money in the quest for happiness and peace. They look for contentment in education, relationships, or even in the church. Yet, some of the most discontented people I have ever met were religious people. They are always looking for the magic faith cure for all of their problems. They put their faith in following formulas that promise the instant solution to whatever they are struggling with. They feel that if you just bang certain Scriptures together and make a lot of noise in praise, then that will chase away all the enemies. However, they try the secret formula, and when it doesn't work the way they wanted, they are left disillusioned and doubting their faith.

The Lord once taught me a lesson about putting my faith in the wrong things. At the time, we were on that little island, pastoring our small church, and living in the church building. We were struggling — making very little money, and living off Hamburger Helper. How is it that Hamburger Helper grows while it's inside the refrigerator? Why is it that when you leave it in there overnight you have more the next day?

I had learned a secret faith formula of prayer that was something like the Prayer of Jabez (1 Chr 4:10) that was popular a few years ago. I put my secret formula to work,[1] trusting the Lord to meet our needs. Whenever things would get really tight, I would put my secret formula to work. Then, I would walk out to the road to get our mail, and to my delight, there would be a check for $1000, which, in the 1980s was a huge amount of money. This happened to us several times — we would get to the bottom, no money left, and then I would pray the secret prayer, run out to the mailbox, and there would be the answer to our faith formula, another $1000 check.

At one point, we really hit rock bottom. So I put the secret faith formula to work again. I ran out to the mailbox, day after day, expecting to find a check, but day after day, nothing came. I prayed, made the positive confession of the faith formula, and

---

1. My secret formula involved the ingredients of claiming a certain promise in the Bible, followed with a positive confession, and sealed with a faith-filled prayer.

waited desperately. As soon as the mailman drove by, I bolted straight for the mailbox, only to find junk mail... and more bills. I was so discouraged. Why wasn't it working? It was then that the small voice of God spoke to me: "Jamie, why don't you just bow down and worship the mail box?" It was both embarrassing and extremely painful (another sprinkler) — I had made an idol out of the formula and the mailbox.[2]

I began to weep. Standing there at my empty mailbox, I began repenting for putting my faith in my faith. I was not trusting the Lord, but using him to get what I wanted. It's not wrong to ask God for specific things and needs, but we cannot pretend to control how and when the Lord will work. We never received another big check in that mailbox, but our God met all of our needs in his own sovereign way.

The Apostle Paul, writing from a prison cell that faith had not delivered him from, wrote of a secret he had discovered. In fact, he borrowed the very words that one of the mysterious religious groups of his day used.[3] Paul said that after over thirty years of walking with Jesus, he had discovered the secret to contentment. In the book of Philippians, Paul declared, "...for I have learned to be content whatever the circumstances. I know what it is to be in need, and I know what it is to have plenty. I have learned the secret of being content in any and every situation, whether well fed or hungry, whether living in plenty or in want. *I can do everything*

---

2. In fact, I was close to starting a new religion called the Postal Fellowship. We could all wear little mailboxes around our necks. We could be seen every day in front of our mailboxes, worshiping, kneeling before the mailbox praying, "O Holy Mailbox, please meet my needs!"

3. This group was called the Stoics, and they believed that the highest virtue that one could attain was complete self-sufficiency — or, to say it in another way, contentment. Paul was going to take this word (and concept) and fill it with new meaning so that it would no longer be self-sufficiency, but Christ-sufficiency.

through him who gives me strength" (Phil 4:11-13, emphasis added). So what is this big secret that Paul discovered? The secret was and is that there is no secret.[4] Paul was saying that there are no formulas, there is no secret knowledge; there is only Jesus. He was mocking the secret religious groups who trusted in their secret knowledge because the truth was not to be found in a secret, but in the open revelation of the Son of God.

Paul didn't find the secret to contentment in himself or in some mysterious spiritual experience. Paul found everything he needed in his relationship with Jesus. This strength that he found in Jesus did not answer all of his questions, remove all of his trials, or protect him from pain like some spiritual good luck charm. No, he found that strength comes from trusting in Jesus and depending on him for everything. It is not about putting our faith in *how* the Lord will do it; it is about trusting him to do it. Paul first had to learn how weak he was, and give up on finding contentment in himself. Paul discovered The Power of Ugly by celebrating his weaknesses so he could receive God's power.

Paul, in his discovery of the strength of weakness, embraced the reality that he could do nothing that pleased God without Christ. He had come to grips with the words of Jesus, "... apart from me you can do nothing ..." (John 15:5). Before Paul got to "I can do everything through him," he surrendered to "I can do nothing without him."

This promise of being able to do all things depends on what God's will is for us, not our will for us. I may want to be the

---

4. J. Oswald Sanders, *Spiritual Maturity: Principles of Spiritual Growth For Every Believer* (Chicago, IL: Moody Press, 1962), 45. A reporter from New York was once sent to discover the secret to the great success of the Evangelist D.L. Moody. His report came back saying that there was no secret, "'I can see nothing whatever in Moody to account for his marvelous work.' When Moody read the report, he chuckled, 'Why, that is the very secret of the movement. There is nothing in it that can explain it but the power of God. The work is God's, not mine.'"

next Michael Jordan, but even after claiming this promise, I will probably still be unable to even touch the net. I can do all things that Jesus has called me to do in his power. I must seek Jesus every day as my "daily bread" (Matt 6:11) to receive the strength to do what he calls me to do.

There are no secrets. It is an open truth that we need Jesus and that without him, we can do nothing that pleases the Father. So bang all the pots and pans you want, but you better put your faith in Jesus, not in the Jabez prayer, the rosary prayer, the postal prayer, or any other formula that someone comes up with.

The Ugly Secret is *trusting Jesus*. Let me give you a simple childlike example of how this secret works. My wife and I took our first sabbatical in thirty years, and had a blast. We laid down our church and went out of town for three months. The hardest part was missing our grandkids. We sent them several letters to keep up with them. One of my grandsons, Ty, who had been living with us before we left, decided to write to Grandpa. Ty was six years old at this time. We had canceled our mail at the house where Ty was living, and were having it forwarded to our cabin in Georgia.

Once a week I would go to the little post office in Clayton to pick up our mail — which was a spiritual experience. I just couldn't wait to get the mail and hear the news from home. As I was looking through the mail, I noticed a white, folded piece of paper with a torn 37-cent stamp (postage was 42 cents) and the words "From Ty." I opened it up to find a photocopied picture of my grandson in his football uniform. I began to weep, right in the middle of that little country post office. All the people around me were probably wondering, "What is wrong with this guy?"

My grandson had discovered the Ugly Secret of trusting Jesus.

He placed a non-addressed letter with insufficient postage and no return address in the mailbox and put up the flag. I can't explain to you how it happened, but the Lord honored Ty's simple trust and delivered the letter to me. When I called Ty later to let him know that I received his letter, his response was, "Of course you did, Grandpa. I mailed it to you."

Ty did not let the facts get in the way of just putting the letter in the mailbox. He figured that everyone in the world knew that he was sending this letter to his grandpa at the "Little Bear Cabin" in Georgia. He did his part the best way that he knew how, and left the rest up to Jesus. The Ugly Secret is that we just need to get "it" into the Lord's hands and he will do the rest. Jesus always delivers! That is the secret of contentment.

This is Paul's mysterious secret that he was "initiated" into, not by a mystical experience, angelic visitation, or supernatural dream, but by shipwreck. This initiation continued through beatings, stoning, persecution, hunger, suffering, and many other trials (2 Cor 11:23-31). Paul learned the Ugly Secret that he could not rely on his own strength, but only on the power of Jesus — with simple childlike trust. This secret may not bring your unfaithful husband home, cure you of cancer, send you a large check in the mail, or fix all of your problems. But it will give you the peace, contentment, and strength to know that God is in control and that you can trust Him, even when you don't understand. If that is not enough for you, then I have nothing else to give you. There are no magic cures for all the problems that we face. I know that this may sound too simple, and it will offend our pride, which demands explanations, but we must come to Jesus as a little child and trust him.

Bishop N. T Wright described this Ugly Secret, when he wrote that the gospel is not an offer for some new, mysterious, cure all experience. "The only experience guaranteed by Jesus' summons is that of carrying the cross."[5]

This Ugly Secret is so simple and clear that we can easily miss it while we are looking for the deep mysteries of the faith. Again, God is hiding his wisdom from the proud and saving it for the little children. Yes, I know it's so easy to say, "Trust in Jesus" or "I can do everything through him who gives me strength," but it takes the miracle of God's grace for us to be able to do it. This secret is simple, but it will cost us dying to our own understanding, and giving up on relying on our own strength — and that is ugly!

---

5. Wright, *What Saint Paul Really Said*, 157.

....

Thus ministry can indeed be a witness to the living
truth that the wound which causes us to suffer now,
will be revealed to us later as the place where God
intimated His new creation.
— Henri Nouwen

Chapter 17. Ugly Scars

Sweetly Broken

I hate hospitals, yet I have been forced to visit them hundreds of times as a pastor. I have spent many long nights in hospitals, but never because I was sick. Why do people feel compelled to show you their scars? They always ask you if you want to see their scars, as their hospital robe is already halfway up. I usually answer "No, thank you," to people who ask if I want to see, but they never listen!

There are many reasons that I never eat at hospitals — there are too many germs around; I've watched too many sick movies about cooking people like *Fried Green Tomatoes*; and mostly because I know someone there is going to expose themselves to me, showing off their Ugly Scars, and I will want to throw up.

My wife and I serve as police chaplains, and one night I was out on a ride-along when we went to a drug arrest. They were arresting a fat guy with a huge beer belly. This guy had cut a half circle out of his shirt, exposing his potbelly, which had a huge, jagged scar on it. He was so proud of it that he needed to show it to everyone! I can only imagine the story behind that scar. You know, you might be a redneck if you cut out clothes to expose your Ugly Scars.

I know that scars are a part of our life stories — knee replacements from too many downhill skiing trips, back surgery from working for years building sea walls, or heart surgery from eating too many one-pounders. Our scars may come from a knife fight over drugs, giving birth through a c-section, a surgery that saved your life, or donating one of your kidneys so your father could live. Scars say, "I made it through. I survived!" They may be ugly, but you're still here, and any scar is better than being a corpse.

"This scar enabled me to walk again."

"This scar gave me my third daughter."

"This scar removed the worst pain imaginable — let me tell you how I got this scar!"

There are several scarred places on my body that I could tell you stories about. I could tell you about scars from motorcycle wrecks, football injuries, or claw hammers stuck in my head; but I want to tell you about the scar I got when I was five years old. My buddy Timmy and I were on a safari adventure trying to capture lizards. After we caught them, we would place them in a glass jar for safekeeping. We had no idea that failing to punch holes in the jar would turn it into a gas chamber for the lizards. After a long day of hunting, we were sitting proudly on our bikes beside each other with our captives held securely in their glass prison. I lost my balance and fell off my bike, knocked my buddy over, and crashed the glass jar on the ground. I landed on the broken glass, and severely cut the palm of my hand — requiring multiple stitches. As I lay there in great pain with my bleeding palm, the lizards escaped to freedom. To this day, there is an entire population of lizards that owe their existence to my sacrifice. I'm sure it may be only a legend, but I have heard of lizards that wear tiny pieces of broken glass around their necks, in honor of the mysterious savior that they refer to as the Lizard King.[1]

Someone has said that Christ followers are either just coming out of a trial, are presently in the middle of one, or are just getting ready to

---

1. I know you may think that Jim Morrison was the first to be called the Lizard King, but he wasn't.

go into one. I find that depressing, but sadly true. I thought that we signed up to follow Jesus to escape problems, avoid jail, be delivered from addictions, find peace, and get a pretty girlfriend. We forgot to read the red on the contract to follow Jesus. In most Bibles, the red words are the words of Jesus. They do this to highlight what Jesus said, and if we read them, it is clearly that to follow him will lead us into much pain, hardship, suffering, persecution, trials, and spiritual attacks from the evil one. Jesus made it crystal clear that we must "... take up ... [the] cross daily and follow ..." him (Luke 9:23). A cross means humbling, suffering, and death. Through this, the cross leads to our "best life" that will not be now, but when Jesus returns and we are resurrected. But who reads the fine print?

I have discovered that Christian lingo has secret code phrases for "life sucks" and they are:

"He is trying my faith."

"He is refining me."

"I am just going through the desert," (which sounds like a rock song to me).

"I'm being persecuted."

"He's teaching me patience."

"He is building character in me."

"It's a dark night of my soul."

"I am in the fiery furnace."

"I'm drinking the cup that he's given me."

"I'm back on the potter's wheel."

We even have worship songs now that speak of God breaking us in a gentle, sweet way.

Let me tell you that this is an oxymoron, and very misleading. If you have ever broken anything, even your pinky toe, it is never sweetly broken! Spiritually, it is no different. To be broken is a horrible, painful, and humiliating experience — and it is never sweet. I don't know if they are attempting to soften the words in red so that we can get more disciples, or if it is just that the writers have not encountered the pruning knife of God, the crushing blow of the potter, or the fire of God purifying us. King David, after experiencing the severe mercy of God's discipline, cried out for God to, "... Let the bones you have *crushed* rejoice" (Ps 51:8, emphasis added). Sweetness can come after brokenness, but it is often after a long, painful process of healing.

We want a soft, padded cross that will not rub us and leave a blister; but Jesus' cross comes with nails. It would be like me writing a song about giving birth just because I have witnessed so many — even though, gratefully, I have never experienced one personally. I could call it: "Sweetly Pushing." Any mother who has ever "pushed" out a bowling ball sized little blessing knows there is no sweetly pushing. It happens amidst screams of, "I can't do this! Give me the drugs!" Or, as Bill Cosby said in *Bill Cosby Himself*, "the second pain hit and my wife... stood up in the stirrups, grabbed my bottom lip and said, 'I want morphine!'"

Yes, the dirty little secret is that the Christian life is painful. Faith is not a magic cure for all of life's troubles. Faith does not provide the way out, but the courage to go through our problems because he is with us. Giving our lives to Jesus invites spiritual assaults, because we realize we are in a spiritual war.

* * *

I was out for one of my power walks[2] one morning while I was in the midst of another intense trial in my life. I was whining and complaining, or if I wanted to act spiritual, I could call it

---

2. I call it power walking because it takes the power of God to get my lazy butt out of my La-Z-Boy. If only using the remote would burn off a bunch of calories!

praying to God. I told God that I agreed with Saint Teresa of Avila when she told him, "If this is the way you treat your friends, it's no wonder you have so few." This raw honesty may offend your religious pride, but it does not offend God. He can deal with our honesty and immaturity with great patience. However, offering up an insincere, fake, religious prayer that is only a performance to impress others with your great spirituality is a stench in his nostrils.

As I was praying through this dark valley, the Lord began to remind me of the story of Jacob[3] who had a brother who wanted to kill him. All his life, Jacob had been a trickster and had been able to get what he wanted by conniving, manipulation, and cleverness. Jacob had come out of the womb wrestling with his twin brother Esau. Jacob's primary weakness was that he was too strong. This is always our greatest danger — our trust in our abilities, resources, and strengths instead of in the grace of God. This is the sin of self-confidence — the sin that most of us are consumed with and blind to, since in our culture this sin is celebrated as a wonderful attribute.

Jacob trusted in his cleverness more than he trusted in God. Now he was in a tight spot with his angry older brother who wanted to kill him for his past deceptions. Jacob even tried praying, but his focus on his fears drove him back to relying on his own strength to defend himself. He began to resort to craftiness again, but God wanted to bring Jacob to the end of himself, stripping him of self-reliance. That night God invited Jacob into the ring for a steel cage match between Jacob and himself. It is not clear if it was an angel, or the pre-incarnate Jesus, but either way, that night God wrestled with Jacob (Gen 32)!

---

3. James, my real name, is Jacob in Hebrew. Jacob means "one who plays tricks," and I have certainly lived up to my name.

I think God loves a good fight! If you read the book of Job, it is God who picks the fight with Satan, because our heavenly Father loves to brag about his kids (Job 1:8). As the Father was bragging about his son Job, it lured the evil one into a fight — with Job at the center. While Job was in the fight of his life, the real battle was going on in the spirit realm — unbeknownst to him.

God is a warrior, and he has never been defeated in battle, except once, in the brief moment when his only Son cried, "... My God, my God, why have you forsaken me" (Matt 27:46)? On that dark day, Jesus chose to lose in order to win. Yet, three days later, Jesus became far greater than the evil one could have ever imagined (Eph 1:20-22).

Our warrior God does have a weakness[4] — it is called mercy, and it can be exploited. People can use it as an excuse to do as they please — mock God, rebel, cover their evil with religion, and wear masks that attempt to hide the truth. Yes, in God's weakness, he is patient and longsuffering. "The Lord is not slow in keeping his promise, as some understand slowness. He is patient with you, not wanting anyone to perish, but everyone to come to repentance" (2 Pet 3:9). I am so grateful for God's weakness and slowness that he did not crush me like a bug or strike me with lightning as I mocked and taunted him in all of my arrogance. God is merciful, but he is also righteous. His justice is coming,[5] but his weakness of mercy continues to cry out in intercession: "Just a little longer. Give them one more chance to repent."

In the weakness of God, he allowed Jacob to wrestle with him to free Jacob of his fears. He did not do this by removing what

---

4. Jesus was "crucified in weakness, yet he lives by God's power." 2 Cor 13:4.

5. But do not be fooled, "the day of the Lord will come like a thief. The heavens will disappear with a roar." 2 Pet 3:10.

Jacob feared, but by bringing him to the end of his own strengths, to a point of surrender, discovering The Power of Ugly — finding God's strength in his weakness. He had to give up on his strengths to overcome these fears. He had to learn to trust and cling to God to defeat his enemies.

It was in this wrestling match with God that Jacob's strength was "Sweetly Broken," yet some will point out that it says Jacob won. Yes, the heavenly man was unable to overpower him, but in God allowing Jacob to win, God touched Jacob's leg and crippled him so that he had to limp for the rest of his life. What Jacob won after his all night wrestling match was what God wanted to give him the whole time — a new name, representing a new character.

He won the name Israel — and he walked with a limp the rest of his life. With great joy he carried the Ugly Scar of being crippled by God. Every step he took with the weakness of his limp reminded him of where his strength came from. He became a stronger man because of his weaknesses. Jacob, now Israel, was always glad to drop his pants and display the Ugly Scar he received from wrestling with his God. This Ugly Scar became a beautiful reminder of how God had hurt him to heal him of his self-reliance.

As this story bounced around in my heart while I was power walking, the Father gave me an impression. I heard him say, "Jamie, you don't get to choose your scars, you only get to choose how you will respond to them." The Lord began to show me that God did not ask Jacob where he wanted to be touched and crippled for the rest of his life. I'm sure if he'd had the choice, he would have given up an ear, arm, or hand, but no one wants to have to live as a cripple. He did not get to pick his scars. He only got to choose how he would respond to them.

Jacob could have left that wrestling match with a bitter heart of self-pity. "Why me? Why my leg? Why do I have to give up so many things I love to do?" Many people respond this way to their undesirable scars. In rejecting their Ugly Scars, they never fully heal. The scars will never bring the hope and restoration to others that God had intended them to bring.

There is no joy in the Father's heart when he sees his children hurt. However, he delights in healing the Ugly Scars in such a way that they become marks of his grace. Healed scars can tell the story of the grace of God so much better than our victory stories!

* * *

A wonderful example of responding to our scars in the right way is provided by one of my heroes — Jay — who is one of the leaders in our church. Jay was a local high school baseball star on his way to receiving an athletic college scholarship, when his whole life changed in a moment. Jay fell asleep while he was at the wheel of his pickup. His truck flipped several times and left him with a broken neck. Jay did not get to pick which vertebra to have broken. Jay would have picked one that left him with the use of his hands, not one that left him as a quadriplegic, restricted to a wheelchair.

It has been over twelve years since Jay had that accident. He is now married to a beautiful lady, who brought with her an adorable little girl. Before they ever met in person, they talked over the Internet for several months. Jay finally found the nerve to tell Alyssa, "If you have not figured it out yet, I have a spinal cord injury that has left me paralyzed." Jay revealed his Ugly Scars with no shame because he had discovered The Power of Ugly. He knew that in spite of his limitations and weaknesses, the Lord was using him greatly. But how would this beautiful young woman that he was falling in love with respond to his Ugly Scars? He held his breath, waiting for a response, for what seemed like an eternity. Seconds later a response popped up on his screen. Alyssa replied, "So what? I'm short."

I have performed many weddings, but none will mean more to me than watching Jay drive his wheelchair down the aisle.[6] Jay did not choose his Ugly Scars, but he has received them, releasing the grace of God to transform them into marks of grace that tell the story of Jesus. In spite of these scars, he runs his own business from home;[7] leads one of our church's community groups; and takes three hours every Sunday to just get out of bed, get dressed, and come to worship with us.

* * *

"Jamie, you don't get to pick your scars." God has put his gentle touch on many areas of my life that I never wanted to be scarred in. I am spiritually covered in Ugly Scars from the all-night wrestling matches that I have had with God. He always lets me win because he wants me to receive my new name and develop the character traits that make me more like Jesus. I know this because of God's weakness, his mercy. After being sweetly broken, I will limp away with a new name and a fresh scar that will tell the story of the grace of God.

Our church is learning to minister to others, not by presenting them with our great strengths and victories, but by lifting up our shirts and exposing our Ugly Scars to tell others the stories of how we have found God's grace in our weakness and ugliness. I

6. He came in to the "blasphemous" (to a Florida Gator fan) fight song of the Ohio State football team.

7. His charity is called "Hands Up," which stands for Helping Acquire Necessary Disability Supplies for Underprivileged People. You can find more information on his website: www.handsupcharity.org

witnessed a beautiful example of this during one of our ministry times at church, as one of our leaders prayed for a pregnant teen that was planning on getting an abortion. Instead of preaching at her, he lifted his shirt and exposed an Ugly Scar from his past. With tears in his eyes, he spoke to her of the pain that he experienced from participating in an abortion years ago. To this day he still wears the emotional scars from that experience, but they have been healed and transformed into scars that tell the story of God's grace. These Ugly Scars saved a life that day; the young girl was so touched that she made the wonderful choice to keep her baby.

This is how we become wounded healers[8] to a world that is filled with suffering. We have accepted the weakness of our strengths, and celebrate the strength of our weaknesses, as they become mighty weapons in the hands of God. Yes, we walk with the limp of grace that reminds us — it is all grace. Every scar tells a story, but a scar that has been healed by his grace tells his story.

So what are your Ugly Scars? I have streaked naked through this book, exposing many of my mine. I have lifted up my shirt without even asking you if you wanted to look. In many ways, I am like the pot-bellied guy with the cut out t-shirt exposing his ugly scar. I have celebrated my weaknesses, failures, and brokenness because I have discovered The Power of Ugly. It is the liberating truth that God loves us in spite of all our uglies! We don't need to wear masks to cover the shame of our brokenness. We can stop hiding and pretending as we try to avoid being seen by God out of fear that he will reject us as others have for our ugliness.

I once saw a redneck sitting at a bar wearing a hat that said, "I Dig Fat Chicks," which I am sure gave hope to someone! God's ball cap declares the good news, "I Love People With Ugly Scars."

---

8. Nouwen, *The Wounded Healer.*

In fact, he loves them so much that he became a "slob just like one of us," so he could lay his life down in weakness to pay for our sins, forever wearing the scars that bring healing to all of our wounds.

Jesus was resurrected still wearing the scars from the nails. Now these scars were completely healed, and he will wear them forever, marking him as the Lamb of God who was slain for us (Rev 5:6). These sacred scars of Jesus represent our healing: "...by his wounds we are healed" (Isa 53:5).

In *The Pilgrims Progress*, John Bunyan writes about Mr. Valiant-for-truth, who, right before he passed from death to life proclaims, "My sword I give to him that shall succeed me in my pilgrimage, and my courage and skill to him that can get it. My marks and scars I carry with me, to be a witness for me that I have fought his battles who now will be my rewarder."[9] I think that Bunyan was on to something, and I have a theory that those scars that come from sacrifices we make in his service or wounds we receive in spiritual battles will be transformed at the resurrection; not removed. We will wear these scars as a warrior would wear a medal — as a badge of honor. Paul alludes to this as he speaks of his scars as "stigmata" or brands or tattoos that mark him as a Christ follower. He is not branded by wearing a gold cross or an ink tattoo, but by wounds from battle in his name.

I believe that those who have been martyred for Jesus will have their mortal wounds transformed into sacred scars that they will forever wear as badges of honor. How else did John, in his vision of heaven, know that the group he saw was made up of "... souls of those who had been slain because of the word of God ..." (Rev 6:9). He was able to recognize them as martyrs because they were still wearing their stigmata (Rev 20:4). Our redeemed scars will forever tell the story of his grace.

---

9. John Bunyan, *The Pilgrim's Progress* (Media Book, Public Domain), 426.

I hope that as I have held up my life in a celebration of ugly, in looking at me, you have seen a glimpse of you. I hope you have found the courage to stop hiding your Ugly Scars and start celebrating them as God covers you with his grace.

* * *

One of my first pastors and a professor of mine in seminary, Dr. Charles Williams, told me of a reoccurring nightmare he had. In the dream he would always end up dying and, to his horror, he would see his tombstone with these words inscribed after his name:

So What?

This gripped him so much that he lived life with a deep commitment to not waste it. He trained me to listen to every sermon, and read every book, with the simple question: *So what? So what* difference does this make in my life? Interesting talk, sermon, or book, but *so what?* How do I apply this? Dr. Williams said that in any good sermon or book, the most important part is the conclusion, the *so what* to whatever you have been saying. *So what* do you want me to do, change, or discover that will make a difference in my life and a difference in the world? So for those of you (like me) who cheat on books by going right to the end to discover the *so what*; and for those of you who flip to the back to see if it is worth spending your money to purchase this book and your time to read it.

Here is my so what:

I am *ugly*. You are *ugly*. The church is *ugly*. We are all *ugly!* Stop hiding it, and start celebrating your weakness. The Apostle Paul wrote, "... I will boast all the more gladly about my weakness [uglies], *so that* Christ's power may rest *on me*" (2 Cor 12:9, emphasis added).

Paul had discovered The Power of Ugly. He wanted God to remove a tormenting pain from his life, but God met him in one of those steel-cage wrestling matches instead. Paul asked God three times to remove his "thorn," (ugliness) but God's response was, "My grace is sufficient for you, *for* my power is made perfect in weakness [ugly]" (2 Cor 12:9, emphasis added). Embrace the ugly weakness of being a human. Stop trying to make yourself perfect, strong, together, and good so that God can love you and use you.

God says, "I pick you, just the way that you are. I pick you in all your insecurities, neurotic hang ups, fears, weaknesses, failures, scars, and shame — in all of your ugliness. I pick you to play on my team, and we will win, but it will be Ugly Winning. I will make an Ugly Exchange with you. I will take your sins, failures, and defeats; and give you my undefeated, perfect Life. I relieve you from pitching; I will strike out all your enemies. I will cover your nakedness. I will receive your Ugly Worship, even when it is filled with grief, pain, disillusionment, and questions — as long as it is all laid at my feet. I will run to you as you begin your journey back to me; I will hug you and kiss you in all of your ugliness. I will cover your brokenness with my best robe. I will use your Ugly Scars to help others who need to discover my grace."

* * *

You are ugly. *So what?* He is beautiful and wants to reveal the wonder of his power through the ugly cracks of your life.

You are ugly. *So what?* He loves to ride on ugly donkeys to enter into his glory. Will you say, "Lord, I will be your ugly donkey?"[10]

You are ugly. *So what?* Dance before him in all of your humanness, weakness, and Ugly Scars. Hear the rhythm of his heart and join in

---

10. I can hear him saying, "Giddy up!"

the Dance of the Broken Bones. Dance even when you can hear the whispers of the religious and the self-righteous saying how undignified and ugly you look. Let the applause of the Audience of One drown out their criticism. Your heavenly Father, who delights in you, will join you in the dance of grace, where our weakness meets his strength, and where our ugly meets his beauty. This is the *so what* of being ugly.

Celebrate being U-G-L-Y because:

Unconditionally

God

Loves

You

And that's beautiful!

"The God and Father of the Lord Jesus, who is to be praised forever, knows that I am not lying" (2 Cor 11:31).
(Well, I may have embellished a little.)

Bibliography

"81-Year-Old Woman Arrested for Urinating in a Park," News One, http://newsone.com/nation/news-one-staff/81-year-old-woman-arrested-for-urinating-in-a-park/ (accessed September 12, 2010).

Assisi, St. Francis of. *Little Flowers of St Francis*, Public Domain.

Bonhoeffer, Dietrich. *Life Together*. San Francisco, CA: Harper San Francisco, 1954.

_____. *The Cost of Discipleship*. New York, NY: Touchstone, 1995.

Brown, Peter. *Augustine of Hippo*. Los Angeles, CA: University of California Press, 2000.

Browning, Elizabeth Barrett. *Aurora Leigh*. London: J. Miller, 1864.

Bunyan, John. The Pilgrim's Progress: Media Book, Public Domain.

Calvin, John. *Institutes of the Christian Religion: Book IV*, Public Domain.

Chambers, Oswald. *My Utmost for His Highest*. New York, NY: Dodd, Mead, and Company, 1935.

Christian, Jayakuma. *God of the Empty-Handed: Poverty, Power & the Kingdom of God*. Monrovia, CA: World Vision International, 1999.

Finney, Charles G. *The Autobiography of Charles G. Finney.* Grand Rapids MI: Bethany House Publishers, 1977.

Gritsch, Eric W. *The Wit of Martin Luther.* Minneapolis, MN: Fortress Press, 2008.

Hybles, Bill. *Just Walk across the Room.* Grand Rapids, MI: Zondervan Publishing Company, 2006.

Leo, Alex, "Man Blames Cat for Child Porn Downloads," The Huffington Post, http://www.huffingtonpost.com/2009/08/13/man-blames-cat-for-child-_n_258752.html (accessed September 11, 2010).

Louv, Richard. *Last Child in the Woods: Saving Our Children from Nature-Deficit Disorder.* Chapel Hill, NC: Algonquin Books, 2008.

Lowney, Chris. *Heroic Leadership.* Chicago, IL: Loyola Press, 2003.

Maraniss, David. *When Pride Still Mattered: A Life of Vince Lombardi.* New York, NY: Simon & Schuster, 2000.

McNeal, Reggie. *A Work of Heart: Understanding How God Shapes Spiritual Leaders.* San Francisco, CA: Jossey-Bass, 2000.

Miller, Donald. *Searching for God Knows What.* Nashville, TN: Nelson Books, 2004.

"Rock of Ages," Music by Augustus M. Toplady, and Words by Thomas Hastings. Public Domain.

Newman, Andy, New York Times, http://www.nytimes.com/2009/02/17/world/americas/17iht-chimp.1.20241928.html (accessed September 12, 2010, 2010).

Nouwen, Henri J. M. *The Wounded Healer: Ministry in Contemporary Society.* New York, NY: Image Books, 1972.

_____. *The Return of the Prodigal Son: A Story of Homecoming.* New York, NY: Image Books, 1994.

Ortberg, John. *Everybody's Normal Till You Get to Know Them.* Grand Rapids, MI: Zondervan, 2003.

Osborne, Joan. *One of Us Relish*: Mercury, 1995.

Owen, John. *The Death of Death in the Death of Christ.* Edinburgh: The Banner of Truth Trust, 1967.

Peterson, Eugene. *Under the Unpredictable Plant.* Grand Rapids, MI: Eerdmans, 1992.

_____. *Leap over a Wall: Earthy Spirituality for Everyday Christians.* New York, NY: Harper Collins, 1998.

_____. *Living the Resurrection.* Colorado Springs, CO: Navpress, 2006.

Puente, Maria. "Why Susan Boyle Inspires Us." USA Today, April 20 2009.

Redman, Matt, "The Heart of Worship," 1997, Kingsway's ThankYou Music,

Sanders, J. Oswald. *Spiritual Maturity: Principles of Spiritual Growth for Every Believer.* Chicago, IL: Moody Press, 1962.

Smith, Bruce. *The World, the Flesh, and Father Smith.* Houghton Mifflin. Boston, MA, 1945.

Smith, L. E. Jr., "Our God Reigns," New Jerusalem Music. 1974, 1978. Used by Permission.

Stewart, Rod. Rhythm of *My Heart Vagabond Heart.* Warner Bros., 1991.

Storms, Sam. *The Singing God.* Orlando, FL: Creation House, 1998.

Stott, John. *Between Two Worlds: The Challenge of Preaching Today.* Grand Rapids, MI: Eerdmans, 1994.

Tozer, A.W. *Worship: The Missing Jewel of the Evangelical Church.* Christian Publications. Worship: The Missing Jewel of the Evangelical Church. Camp. Hill, PA: Christian Publications, n.d.

Vanauken, Sheldon. *A Severe Mercy*. New York, NY: Harper and Row, 1977.

Wagner, C. Peter. *How to Have a Healing Ministry Without Making Your Church Sick*. Ventura, CA: Gospel Light, 1988.

Wimber, John. *The Way In is the Way On*. Atlanta, GA: Ampelon Publishing, 2006.

_____. *Everyone Gets to Play*. Atlanta, GA: Ampelon Publishing, 2008.

Wolfe, Tom. *The Electric Kool-Aid Acid Test*. New York, NY: Bantam Books, 1980.

"In the Garden." Words and Music by Austin Miles. Public Domain.

Wright, N.T. *What Saint Paul Really Said: Was Paul of Tarsus the Real Founder of Christianity?* Grand Rapids, MI: Eerdmans, 1997.

_____. *Surprised by Hope: Rethinking Heaven, the Resurrection, and the Mission of the Church*. New York, NY: Harper One, 2008.

Yaconelli, Michael. *Messy Spirituality*. Grand Rapids, MI: Zondervan Publishing Co., 2007.

Yancey, Philip. *What's So Amazing About Grace?* Grand Rapids, MI: Zondervan Publishing Co., 1997.

_____. *Soul Survivor*. New York, NY: Galilee, 2001.

_____. *Living the Resurrection*. Colorado Springs, CO: Navpress, 2006.